The Ultimate Generative AI Guidebook

How Anyone Can Master Advanced AI Concepts and Practical Applications Stress-Free

Jordan Blake

Table of Contents

Introduction

The rapid ascent of generative AI is nothing short of a technological revolution, touching everything from the way we manage patient care in healthcare to how we generate new content in the entertainment industry. Its capacity to boost creativity, enhance efficiency, and elevate problem-solving reshapes landscapes across the board.

My journey into the world of AI began unexpectedly during my sophomore year in college when I attended a workshop on neural networks. It was there, amidst lines of code and lively discussions about the future of technology, that I first witnessed a generative AI model in action. The model took a simple concept and transformed it into a complex, beautifully detailed graphic design. This experience didn't just pique my interest—it redirected my career path and ignited a passion for AI that has driven me ever since.

This book is crafted to peel back the layers of generative AI, making it approachable and engaging not only for tech professionals but also for enthusiasts and beginners who are curious about this field. I aim to simplify advanced AI concepts and their practical applications, enabling you to apply these techniques in real-world scenarios, whether you are a student, a developer, or simply an AI aficionado.

Designed with you in mind, this guide is perfect for anyone ranging from college students to seasoned tech professionals interested in integrating generative AI into their work or hobbies. By starting with the foundational terms and progressively moving to more complex applications, the book ensures that you build a robust understanding of both the basics and the intricacies of generative AI.

Recognizing the importance of hands-on learning, I've included step-by-step guides, real-world examples, and engaging activities that not only enhance your comprehension but also encourage you to apply what you learn. Each chapter builds upon the previous one, ensuring a structured learning curve that prepares you to tackle advanced concepts with confidence.

Ethical considerations are paramount in AI development and application. This book dedicates a section to discussing the ethical implications of generative AI, ensuring that as you grow in your understanding and ability to create with AI, you are also equipped to think critically about its impacts.

To enrich your learning experience, the book includes links to additional online resources, interactive projects, and practical examples. These elements are designed to provide you with the opportunity to explore concepts in depth and apply your knowledge in dynamic ways.

As we stand on the brink of unprecedented innovation with generative AI, I invite you to join this exciting journey. Embrace this technology as a theoretical study and a practical tool to drive creativity and innovation in your career and daily life. The future of generative AI is bright and full of potential, and by engaging with this book, you are stepping into a world of immense possibilities.

Let's explore this transformative technology together, unlocking new opportunities and pioneering advancements in the field of artificial intelligence. Together, we can shape a future where generative AI not only enhances our professional capabilities but also enriches our personal lives.

FOUNDATIONS OF
GENERATIVE AI

Chapter 1:

Foundations of Generative AI

When you first hear "generative AI," you might think it's a fancy term cooked up in a Silicon Valley boardroom to dazzle investors. But in reality, it's a lot more down-to-earth and far-reaching than that. Generative AI isn't just a buzzword; it's a pivotal force in the tech landscape, propelling industries from mundane to miraculous transformations. Whether you're remixing beats for a new pop hit or designing custom sneakers from a sketch, generative AI is the invisible hand guiding these creative processes.

Now, let's talk about my first brush with this technology. During a hackathon in my junior year, I stumbled upon a team working on a generative AI project for creating digital art. I was mesmerized—not just by the technology, but by the way it could take a simple doodle and turn it into gallery-worthy artwork. It was then that I realized: This tech was more than lines of code; it was a bridge to a world where technology meets creativity.

1.1 Demystifying Generative AI: An Introduction

What Exactly Is Generative AI?

To kick things off, let's clarify what we mean by "generative AI". This technology involves algorithms that can learn from existing data and then use that learning to generate new content—be it text, images, sounds, or nearly anything else within the digital realm. The magic here is not just replication but its ability to innovate, creating something entirely new from what it has learned.

Now, contrast this with discriminative models, which are the hallmarks of traditional AI. Think of discriminative algorithms as meticulous critics—they analyze data to categorize or make predictions. For example, a convolutional neural network (CNN) excels in image recognition tasks, identifying objects within an image. On the flip side, generative adversarial networks (GANs), a type of generative AI, are like imaginative artists. A GAN consists of two parts: a generator that creates images and a discriminator that critiques these images. Through their rivalry, the generator learns to produce increasingly sophisticated outputs.

Tracing the Roots and Rise of Generative AI

The journey of generative AI began in the quieter corners of academia with simple neural networks and has since soared to the forefront of AI innovation. The real game changer was the development of GANs in 2014, which showed us that machines could not only learn but could also be creatively independent. Fast forward to the introduction of transformers in 2017, and we entered a new era where machines could handle language with a finesse that was previously the sole domain of humans. These milestones aren't just academic—they're the foundation stones of the modern AI landscape.

Generative AI at Work: Applications and Implications

The real-world applications of generative AI are as diverse as they are impactful. In the entertainment industry, it's transforming how we create and interact with media. From AI-driven film scripts to personalized video games, the creative boundaries are continually expanding. In healthcare, generative AI assists in drug discovery by predicting molecular reactions, potentially speeding up the development of new treatments.

But that's just scratching the surface. The implications of these applications are profound, offering not only commercial benefits but also enhancing our ability to solve complex problems across sectors. As these technologies evolve, they could redefine the limits of human creativity and ingenuity.

What's in Store?

As we navigate through this book, expect to unravel how generative AI operates across different scenarios, from simple applications to complex systems that mimic human intelligence. You'll gain more than an understanding of the technology; you'll walk away with practical skills to implement AI solutions. Whether you're a seasoned developer or a curious newbie, the content is structured to provide a comprehensive understanding without overwhelming you.

Ethical Considerations: A Primer

Before we dive deeper, it's crucial to touch on the ethical landscape of generative AI. As much as it serves as a powerful tool for innovation, its capabilities come with significant responsibilities. From privacy concerns in data usage to the potential for misuse in creating deceptive media, the ethical implications are wide-ranging. This book will explore these aspects, emphasizing the importance of developing and using AI technologies responsibly.

Engage and Innovate

This book is peppered with interactive elements to ensure that you're not just passively absorbing information. Web links are embedded throughout, leading you to simulations and projects that allow you to experiment with generative AI firsthand. These activities are designed to reinforce your learning and inspire you to think about how you can apply generative AI in your own projects and careers.

As we set the stage for a deep dive into the world of generative AI, remember that this technology is not just about understanding algorithms—it's about envisioning and building a future that leverages AI to its fullest potential. So, gear up: We're just getting started.

1.2 A Deep Dive Into Neural Networks and Their Mechanisms

When we peel back the layers of the marvel that is artificial intelligence, at its core, you'll find neural networks. Think of them as the brain's digital cousins—complex yet fascinating. Neural networks are essentially a web of neurons, not unlike the human brain, designed to recognize patterns and solve problems, but let's not get ahead of ourselves. First, let's break down the architecture of these networks. At the most basic level, a neural network consists of layers of neurons: an input layer, hidden layers, and an output layer. Each neuron in these layers is connected to several others and includes an activation function that determines whether and how strongly to fire, based on the inputs it receives. This setup allows the network to handle everything from simple to highly complex tasks, from recognizing your face in a photo to translating languages in real time.

To understand how these networks learn, let's talk about backpropagation and gradient descent—two processes as crucial to AI as coffee is to programmers during a midnight coding sprint. Backpropagation is the network's way of learning from its mistakes. It adjusts its weights based on the errors in its predictions, moving backwards from the output to the input layer—hence the name. Coupled with gradient descent, a method that minimizes the error by updating the weights in the direction that decreases the error most rapidly, these processes ensure that the network learns accurately and improves over time. Imagine you're trying to teach a dog new tricks; you change your methods based on what works and what doesn't, continually refining your approach. That's essentially what backpropagation and gradient descent do for neural networks.

Now, not all neural networks are created equal. Consider convolutional neural networks (CNNs), which are like the sharpshooters of the AI world, excelling in picking out patterns in images. They're structured specifically to process pixel data and use filters to identify things like edges in an image, making them invaluable in fields like medical imaging and autonomous driving. On the other hand, recurrent neural networks (RNNs) shine in handling sequences, such as spoken language or written texts. They have a kind of memory that allows them to remember previous inputs in the sequence, making them ideal for tasks like speech recognition or language translation. Then there are autoencoders, unsung heroes designed to compress and then decompress data, essentially learning to ignore noise and focus on the most significant features.

However, the path to training these networks isn't without its hurdles. Overfitting is a common challenge that occurs when a model learns the training data, including its noise and inaccuracies, too well. It's like memorizing answers for a test without understanding the underlying principles, which doesn't end well when faced with new questions. Vanishing gradients, another issue, occur when gradients become too small, effectively stopping the network from learning further. This can be likened to a car running out of gas on a long journey—progress stalls. To combat these issues, techniques such as dropout, where randomly selected neurons are ignored during training, or using ReLU (Rectified Linear Unit) activation functions to keep gradients from vanishing, are employed. These strategies help ensure that neural networks don't just memorize but truly learn, adapting to new and unseen data effectively.

By understanding and manipulating these intricate systems, we unlock immense potential across various sectors. Whether it's aiding doctors in diagnosing diseases or helping cars understand the world around them, neural networks are at the forefront, driving progress in ways that were once the realm of science fiction. As we dive deeper into the capabilities and applications of these networks, it becomes clear that we're not just observers but active participants in this era of rapid technological advancement. Let's continue to explore and push the boundaries of what these digital brains can achieve.

Experiment with neural networks on the TensorFlow Playground:

1.3 Understanding Transformers and Their Role in AI

Imagine stepping into a gallery where each painting seamlessly morphs into the next, each brushstroke informed by the ones that came before yet predicting the hues and forms of those to follow. This is somewhat akin to the mechanism driving the transformer models in AI, representing a significant evolution from their predecessors like RNNs (recurrent neural networks). Unlike RNNs, which process data sequentially, thus suffering from slow training times and difficulty in capturing longer dependencies in data, transformers revolutionize this by operating on entire sequences simultaneously. This is made possible through a mechanism known as self-attention, a clever method that allows each position in the sequence to attend to all positions in the previous layer simultaneously.

To dissect this further, let's look at BERT (Bidirectional Encoder Representations from Transformers) and GPT (Generative Pretrained Transformer), two landmark models that have set new standards in natural language processing (NLP) tasks. BERT, designed to pre-train deep bidirectional representations, fundamentally changes the game by conditioning on both left and right context in all layers. As a result, the model is pre-trained on a large corpus of text and then fine-tuned for specific tasks, allowing it to achieve remarkable success in tasks like question answering and language inference. On the flip side, GPT flips the script by using a left-to-right approach, where each token—or unit of data—can only attend to previously generated tokens in the autoregressive task. This mechanism has proven to be a powerhouse in generating coherent and contextually rich text, pushing the boundaries of what AI can generate creatively.

The real magic of transformers, however, lies in their scalability and efficiency. Thanks to their ability to process data points in parallel rather than sequentially, transformers are uniquely suited for handling large datasets—a typical scenario in the age of big data. This parallel processing capability not only speeds up the training process but also improves the performance of these models as they scale. In an era where data is king, the ability of transformers to train on vast amounts of information efficiently is a game changer, making them ideal for tasks that involve understanding and generating human-like text across various languages and contexts.

Current research and advancements in transformer technology continue to push the envelope, exploring new paradigms in AI. One exciting area of research is the integration of transformers with other types of neural networks to enhance their capabilities and efficiency. For example, researchers are experimenting with hybrid models that combine CNNs and transformers to process visual data, leveraging the spatial hierarchy of CNNs and the powerful sequence modeling of transformers. Another promising direction is the development of sparse transformers, which aim to reduce the computation required for training and inference without sacrificing performance. These models use a sparse version of the attention mechanism to focus on a subset of relevant tokens, significantly speeding up processing times and making transformers even more scalable.

As we continue to chart the course of AI development, the transformer model stands out as a beacon of innovation, guiding us toward more efficient, scalable, and effective solutions. The implications of this technology are profound, influencing both the field of AI and the industries it permeates. From automated customer service systems to advanced language translation services, the potential applications of transformers are vast and varied, hinting at an AI-driven future that is not only possible but is rapidly becoming a reality. As these models evolve, they promise to unlock new capabilities and opportunities across sectors, redefining what machines can achieve and how they interact with the world around them. The journey of exploring and optimizing transformers is just beginning, and it's one that promises to be as transformative as the technology itself.

1.4 The Basics of Large Language Models (LLMs)

In the expansive universe of artificial intelligence, large language models (LLMs) are akin to the linguistic savants of the digital world. These models, which include titans like OpenAI's GPT series, are designed to understand and generate human-like text by digesting vast amounts of digital text. LLMs are not just about parsing or generating mundane text; they're about creating text that's as nuanced and fluent as what you'd expect from a seasoned writer. This capability not only makes them fascinating but also incredibly powerful tools across various sectors.

Training these behemoths is no small feat. It involves feeding them diverse datasets comprising an extensive array of text sources—from books and articles to websites and other media. This training enables the models to learn the intricacies of language, including grammar, context, and even the subtleties of cultural references. For instance, OpenAI's GPT-3, one of the most advanced LLMs to date, was trained on a dataset that's a mixture of licensed data, data created by human trainers, and publicly available data. This robust training process allows GPT-3 to generate text that can be astonishingly coherent and contextually appropriate, tackling anything from writing poetry to simulating dialogues.

The applications of LLMs are as broad as they are impactful. In the customer service sector, LLMs power sophisticated chatbots that handle inquiries and provide support with a level of sophistication that can rival human operators. In content generation, these models assist in crafting everything from catchy advertising copy to deep, thought-provoking articles on a myriad of subjects. Furthermore, LLMs are making significant inroads in education technology, where they personalize learning content for students based on their learning history and preferences, thereby enhancing the learning experience and educational outcomes.

However, the power of LLMs comes with its set of challenges, particularly concerning bias and ethical use. Like all machine learning models, LLMs learn from the data they are fed. If this data contains biases—which it often does—the model will likely perpetuate or even amplify these biases in its outputs. This can have serious implications, from reinforcing stereotypes to misinforming users, depending on how the generated content is used. Moreover, the opacity of LLMs, which are often referred to as "black box" models due to their complex and inscrutable nature, makes it difficult to diagnose and correct biases.

Addressing these challenges requires a multifaceted approach. One way to mitigate bias is by diversifying the training datasets, ensuring they represent a wide range of demographics, cultures, and viewpoints. Additionally, ongoing monitoring and tweaking of the models are essential to identify and address biases that may not have been evident during initial training. Another approach is implementing more transparent model architectures or explanation layers that can help developers and users understand how the model arrived at a particular output, thus increasing trust and manageability.

As we integrate LLMs more deeply into our digital ecosystems, their role in shaping communication, content creation, and interaction will only grow. Their ability to understand and generate human-like text makes them invaluable, but it also bestows a great responsibility on those who develop and deploy them. By tackling the associated challenges head-on, we can harness the benefits of LLMs while minimizing their risks, paving the way for more innovative, inclusive, and ethical applications in the future. This journey through the capabilities and complexities of LLMs is not just about understanding a piece of technology; it allows us to envision and craft the future of communication and interaction in an increasingly AI-driven world.

1.5 Generative Adversarial Networks (GANs): What You Need to Know

Imagine two artists in a spirited paint-off, where one sketches a scene and the other critiques it, pushing the first to refine their strokes until the critic can no longer distinguish the painting from a real photograph. This is the essence of generative adversarial networks (GANs), a fascinating framework in AI that pits two neural networks—a generator and a discriminator—against each other. The generator's job is to create, much like our artist, while the discriminator evaluates the creations, playing the role of the art critic. This competitive setup enables the generator to produce increasingly sophisticated outputs, improving through the iterative feedback from the discriminator.

Let's delve a bit deeper into this dynamic duo's roles. The generator starts with a random input and attempts to generate an output that resembles the training data. This output then goes to the discriminator, which tries to determine whether the input it receives is a "fake" from the generator or a "real" from the actual dataset. The fascinating part? The discriminator's feedback loops back to the generator, which uses it to improve its next output. The cycle continues until the discriminator can hardly tell the difference between real and generated outputs, indicating that the generator has mastered mimicking the training data.

The practical applications of GANs are as riveting as their architecture. In the realm of image generation and enhancement, GANs are doing wonders. They can take a sketch and transform it into photorealistic images or take a low-resolution image and enhance it to high definition, which is a boon for fields ranging from forensic science to fashion and design. Style transfer, another intriguing application, allows GANs to apply the style of one image, say a Van Gogh painting, to the subject of another, effectively enabling users to create new artworks with distinctive artistic influences without needing to wield a paintbrush.

However, training GANs is not without its challenges. One of the most notorious issues is mode collapse, where the generator starts producing a limited variety of outputs, or even the same output over and over, instead of a diverse range that truly mimics the training data. This happens when the generator finds a particular form of output that consistently fools the discriminator and then keeps tweaking it slightly in every iteration, leading to stagnation in learning. To combat this, techniques such as minibatch discrimination—where the discriminator assesses a batch of outputs instead of one at a time—help in promoting variety in the generated outputs. Another method involves periodically resetting the discriminator to prevent it from overpowering the generator too early in the training process.

Beyond technical hurdles, the ethical implications of GAN technology stir up significant debate. The power of GANs to create convincing fake images and videos leads to concerns about their use in generating deepfakes, which can have serious consequences in areas like politics, security, and personal privacy. The creation of realistic yet entirely fictional images of people can lead to misuse in the form of fraud, defamation, or manipulation. Addressing these concerns requires stringent ethical guidelines and robust mechanisms to prevent misuse. Transparency in the use of GAN-generated images and videos, clear labeling, and perhaps even the development of technology to detect deepfakes are crucial steps toward responsible deployment of this powerful AI capability.

In the expansive realm of AI technologies, GANs represent both a remarkable advancement and a cautionary tale. Their ability to learn and create from competition mirrors not just a technical process but a fundamentally human pursuit—striving to improve through challenge and feedback. As we continue to explore the capabilities and impacts of

GANs, the journey promises to be as dynamic and evolving as the technology itself.

Experiment with FreeFlo's reusable AI style prompts that use the power of GAN to create captivating images:

1.6 Key Algorithms That Power Generative AI

Diving into the engine room of generative AI, we find an array of sophisticated algorithms, each playing a pivotal role in shaping the landscape of artificial intelligence. Among these, Markov chains, Monte Carlo methods, and variational autoencoders stand out as foundational pillars that support a wide range of generative applications. Understanding these algorithms isn't just about adding tools to your tech toolkit; it's about uncovering new ways to think about problem-solving in the digital age.

Let's start with Markov chains. These are mathematical systems that hop from one "state" (a situation or set of values) to another. It's kind of like playing a board game where each roll of the dice moves you to a new position with its own set of possibilities and outcomes. In the realm of generative AI, Markov chains are used for their predictive prowess. They are particularly famous for their application in text generation, where each word generated is dependent on the previous word, forming a chain of word sequences that can construct everything from poetic verses to entire speeches. Here's a simple pseudocode snippet that illustrates how a Markov chain might be programmed to generate text:

```
function generateText(wordList, chainLength):

        index = random(0, len(wordList) - 1)

        result = []

        for i in 0 to chainLength:

        result.append(wordList[index])

        index = (index + 1) % len(wordList)

        return result
```

This function initializes at a random point in a list of words and generates a sequence of a specified length where each word follows the next in order. The simplicity of Markov chains makes them not only easy to understand but also surprisingly powerful in stitching together coherent sequences from a dataset of possibilities.

Moving on, Monte Carlo methods are your go-to algorithm when you need to crack problems that seem to defy deterministic solutions. These methods use randomness to yield results that might be deterministic in principle. They're like making an educated guess, but these guesses are backed by the power of computation and probability. In generative AI, Monte Carlo methods are often used in optimization and numerical integration, particularly in scenarios where the dataset is vast, and the dimensions are too complex for traditional analysis. For instance, they can simulate the probability of different outcomes in financial forecasting or risk assessment, providing insights that help in making data-driven decisions. The strength of Monte Carlo methods lies in their versatility and robustness, especially in stochastic problem-solving.

Lastly, let's talk about variational autoencoders (VAEs). These are powerful algorithms used for data encoding and generation. Imagine you have a noisy dataset, like photographs where each image is slightly blurred. VAEs can learn to encode this data into a cleaner, compact representation, and then decode it back into an output that retains the original characteristics minus the noise. Here's a bit of pseudocode to illustrate:

```
function variationalAutoencoder(data):

    encoded = encode(data)

    decoded = decode(encoded)

    return decoded
```

In this function, data is input into an encoder to produce a compressed representation, which is then decoded back into its original form. The practical applications of VAEs extend beyond image processing; they are also used in anomaly detection, where they can identify data points that deviate significantly from the norm.

Each of these algorithms has its strengths and limitations. Markov chains, for example, are incredibly efficient with sequential data but can oversimplify complex processes. Monte Carlo methods offer powerful solutions for numerical problems but can be computationally expensive and slow. VAEs provide excellent results in data compression and generation but can be challenging to train and require a substantial amount of data to perform well.

By integrating these algorithms into your projects, you can leverage their unique capabilities to enhance model performance and tackle a wide range of problems in generative AI. Whether you're generating new data, optimizing processes, or decoding complex datasets, these algorithms offer a gateway to innovative solutions and applications. As you continue to explore the vast possibilities of generative AI, remember that these algorithms are not just tools but catalysts that can transform the theoretical into the tangible, opening up a world of opportunities in technology and beyond.

ADVANCED CONCEPTS IN GENERATIVE AI

Chapter 2:

Advanced Concepts in Generative AI

Welcome to the dojo of generative AI, where we dive into the intricacies that make machines not just think but think smartly. If you thought understanding your in-laws was complex, brace yourself; these AI concepts are about to take "complex" to a whole new level. But fear not, we'll break it down with the finesse of a master chef fileting a fish—smooth, precise, and seemingly effortless.

2.1 Exploring Attention Mechanisms in Depth

The Mechanics of Attention: More than Just a Glance

Imagine you're at a bustling party, full of guests chattering away. Amidst this cacophony, your brain remarkably tunes into a specific conversation about the latest tech gadget that piques your interest. This ability to focus on particular sounds while ignoring others is akin to what attention mechanisms in AI accomplish. In the digital realm, these mechanisms enable models to focus on relevant parts of the input data, significantly enhancing the efficiency and accuracy of tasks such as translation and summarization.

At its core, an attention mechanism in AI models recalibrates the focus on input features that are crucial for performing a specific task. For instance, in a language translation task, the model learns to pay more attention to subject-verb agreements in sentences, ensuring grammatical accuracy in the translated output. This selective attention not only improves task performance but also speeds up the processing time, as the model isn't wastefully pondering over irrelevant data.

Spotlight on Different Types of Attention

Diving deeper, let's explore the gallery of attention types—each a masterpiece with its unique flair. First up is self-attention, a mechanism that allows inputs to interact with each other (think of how different words in a sentence affect each other's context). This type is brilliantly utilized in models like transformers that handle tasks requiring a deep understanding of language context.

Next, we encounter multi-headed attention—a beast with multiple heads, each looking in a different direction. This type allows the model to attentively consider information from various representation subspaces at different positions simultaneously. It's like having a team of experts focusing on different aspects of a problem, from syntax to sentiment, to ensure a comprehensive understanding.

To illustrate, imagine a scenario where a model uses multi-headed attention to process a sentence like "The trophy doesn't fit in the suitcase because it's too large." The model efficiently determines that "it" refers to the trophy and not the suitcase, a nuance that less sophisticated models might miss.

Linking Attention to Performance Enhancements

The proof is in the pudding—or in this case, the performance metrics. Attention mechanisms have been revolutionary, propelling models to achieve state-of-the-art results across multiple domains. For example, in machine translation, models equipped with attention mechanisms have significantly outperformed their predecessors, delivering more accurate and contextually appropriate translations.

A case in point is the transformer model, which has leveraged attention mechanisms to great effect, setting new benchmarks in not just language tasks but also in areas like image processing and even music generation. These models, through focused computational power, can generate complex outputs that were previously out of reach for machines.

Scaling and Optimizing Attention Mechanisms

However, with great power comes great computational responsibility. Scaling attention mechanisms can be akin to tuning a high-performance sports car—it's not just about speed but also about efficiency. One of the main challenges lies in managing computational resources, as attention mechanisms, especially in large models, can be resource intensive.

Strategies for optimization include techniques such as pruning, where less important connections are trimmed, much like cutting away dead branches on a plant to help it grow better. Another approach is quantization, which reduces the precision of the numbers used in the model, thus decreasing the memory usage without a substantial loss in performance.

By integrating these strategies, we can scale attention-equipped models more effectively, making them not only powerful but also practical for use in real-world applications across industries. From powering real-time language translators to aiding in complex medical diagnoses, optimized attention mechanisms are setting the stage for an AI-driven future that's not just smart but also efficient and scalable.

As we continue to unravel the mysteries and potentials of attention in AI, remember that this journey is about fostering a deeper understanding and appreciation for the nuances that make these technologies not just function but excel. Let's keep our attention focused on pushing the boundaries of what's possible, one algorithm at a time.

Explore how attention mechanisms can perform advanced text analysis with IBM Watson's Natural Language Processing demo:

2.2 The Evolution of Autoencoders in Data Compression

Imagine a world where the clutter of raw data could be neatly folded away like clothes in a Marie Kondo-inspired dresser. That's the essence of what autoencoders do in the realm of data compression. Tracing back to their inception, autoencoders started as relatively simple neural networks used primarily for reducing data dimensionality. Initially, their role was straightforward: compress data into a smaller, more manageable form without losing critical information, akin to packing your most essential belongings into a suitcase for an extended trip.

Over time, as the digital universe expanded, the demands on autoencoders grew. The evolution saw the birth of more sophisticated variants, such as variational autoencoders (VAEs), which compressed data and generated new data points based on the learned representations. This shift marked a significant milestone, turning autoencoders from mere data compressors into creators capable of contributing to generative models in AI. The development of these advanced autoencoders has been pivotal, particularly in their ability to handle and make sense of vast amounts of unstructured data, paving the way for innovations in machine learning and beyond.

Autoencoders and the Art of Noise Reduction

In the bustling world of digital information, noise is an inevitable guest. Whether it's unwanted distortions in images or background buzz in audio recordings, noise can distort the clarity and quality of data. Here, autoencoders play a crucial role in denoising, which involves filtering out the noise to enhance data quality. The process is somewhat reminiscent of using a sieve to separate flour from unwanted lumps, ensuring only the finest grains (or data) are used for cooking (or analysis).

For instance, consider an image with pixel-level distortions. An autoencoder can learn to recognize and reconstruct the essential features of the image, minimizing the impact of the noise. This capability does more than improve aesthetics; it also enhances the performance of other machine learning models by providing cleaner, more accurate data. Before-and-after examples in image processing clearly show how autoencoders can transform a grainy, indistinct photo into a sharper, clearer image, much like how a restorer might clean centuries of grime from a once-vibrant painting

Diving Deep Into Variational Autoencoders (VAEs)

While traditional autoencoders are adept at compression, variational autoencoders take a leap further into the generative domain. What sets VAEs apart is their foundation in probability theory. Unlike standard autoencoders that encode an input into a fixed point, VAEs encode inputs into distributions—each defined by means and variances. This approach allows VAEs to compress and generate new data points, effectively capturing the essence of the input data in a way that can be tweaked and sampled for new creations.

The magic of VAEs lies in their ability to handle uncertainty and variability, making them incredibly powerful for tasks where modeling complex distributions is crucial. For example, in the pharmaceutical industry, VAEs can help in drug discovery by generating novel molecular structures. These models provide a probabilistic manner to explore chemical spaces that might be infeasible for humans to calculate manually.

Beyond Compression: Autoencoders in Anomaly Detection and Feature Learning

The utility of autoencoders extends beyond the realms of mere data compression into the territories of anomaly detection and feature learning. In anomaly detection, autoencoders can learn to represent normal behavior and, in doing so, can identify deviations or anomalies by noting when data points do not compress well according to the learned representations. This application is crucial in scenarios like fraud detection in finance or fault detection in manufacturing, where recognizing outliers can prevent costly errors.

Feature learning, another critical application, involves using autoencoders to uncover and learn useful representations from data automatically. These features can then be used to improve the performance of predictive models. For instance, in face recognition technologies, autoencoders can help extract features that are robust to variations in lighting or facial expressions, thereby enhancing the accuracy and reliability of the recognition systems.

As we explore these advanced applications of autoencoders, we begin to appreciate their versatility and potential in shaping the future of AI. From compressing data and enhancing images to detecting anomalies and generating new data points, autoencoders demonstrate a remarkable capacity to adapt and excel in a variety of challenging environments. Their evolution from simple compression tools to complex, generative models highlights a journey of growth and transformation, mirroring the dynamic landscape of artificial intelligence itself. As they continue to evolve, autoencoders not only redefine the limits of data compression but also continue to unlock new possibilities across diverse domains, heralding a new era of innovation in AI.

2.3 Transformer Architectures and Beyond

In the bustling bazaar of AI innovations, transformer architectures have been akin to a blockbuster store opening—drawing crowds and setting new trends. But as with any pioneering product, the initial dazzle doesn't preclude the arrival of next-gen improvements. Architectures like Transformer-XL and Reformer are not just iterating on their predecessor's success but are redefining efficiency in profound ways.

Transformer-XL leaps over one of the main hurdles faced by standard transformers: handling longer sequences of data. Traditional transformers, for all their merits, struggle with long-term dependencies primarily due. This is akin to reading a novel and trying to remember plot details several chapters back without flipping the pages again. Transformer-XL addresses this by using a segment-level recurrence mechanism and a state reuse strategy, which allows it to learn dependencies beyond its fixed-length context. This enhancement boosts performance on tasks involving extended sequences, such as document classification or novel-length text generation, and it does so with remarkable efficiency in computational resource usage.

On another front, the Reformer tackles the issue of memory consumption head-on. Transformers are notorious for their appetite for RAM, especially when trained on lengthy sequences. The Reformer changes the game by introducing two key innovations: locality-sensitive hashing, which reduces the complexity of attention from quadratic to linear, and reversible residual layers, which allow for storage of significantly fewer intermediate values during training. These features make the Reformer not just leaner in terms of memory usage but also faster, enabling the training of models on even longer sequences and larger datasets without necessitating a supercomputer.

The evolution doesn't stop here. Hybrid models are emerging, blending the strengths of transformers with other neural network architectures to create something greater than the sum of their parts. For instance, imagine combining the contextual prowess of transformers with the image-processing power of convolutional neural networks (CNNs). This hybrid could excel in tasks that require understanding the nuances of both text and visual data, such as automatic video captioning or multimodal translation services. These models leverage the transformer's ability to handle sequential data and CNN's capacity to process spatial information, providing a holistic approach to problems that involve diverse data types.

Looking to the horizon, the potential trajectories for transformer technology are as varied as they are exciting. One promising avenue is the integration of transformers in reinforcement learning environments. Here, transformers could enhance decision-making processes by better understanding sequences of actions and their outcomes. Another burgeoning area is the use of transformers in edge computing devices, where efficiency and speed are paramount. As these models become more resource-efficient, their deployment in real-time applications, such as on smartphones or in autonomous vehicles, becomes increasingly feasible.

The continuous innovation in transformer architectures is not just expanding their applicability but also challenging our expectations of what machines can comprehend and accomplish. From enhancing linguistic fluency to understanding the subtleties of human emotions in conversations, the advancements in these architectures are setting the stage for an era where AI's integration into daily life is seamless and intuitive. As we forge ahead, the evolution of these models will likely keep us on our toes, eagerly anticipating the next breakthrough that will once again shift the boundaries of possibility in the realm of artificial intelligence.

2.4 Sequence-to-Sequence Models for Advanced Text Generation

In the dynamic world of AI, sequence-to-sequence models are like skilled linguists of machine learning, adept at translating not just languages but also converting any sequence-based information from one form to another. These models are crucial in tasks that involve a transformation of input sequences into output sequences, where both the input and output can be phrases, sentences, or even longer text forms. This capability makes them indispensable in a variety of applications, from machine translation and speech recognition to chatbot functionality and automated summarization.

At its core, a sequence-to-sequence model features a dual-component architecture known as the encoder-decoder structure. Here's how it works: The encoder processes the input sequence, be it text, audio, or any sequential data, and compresses this entire input into a fixed size "context vector". This vector, a dense encapsulation of the input sequence's information, serves as a compressed representation from which the decoder generates the output sequence. Think of the encoder as someone who distills a detailed story into a synopsis, which the decoder then uses to retell the story in a different style or language. This process extends beyond simple translation to involve understanding and retaining the context and nuances of the original input, ensuring that the output is both accurate and contextually relevant.

Advanced Optimizations: Enhancing the Magic

To boost the efficiency and effectiveness of sequence-to-sequence models, several advanced optimization techniques are employed. Beam search is one such technique that enhances the decision-making process during the generation of the output sequence. Unlike a greedy search that selects the most probable next step, beam search considers multiple possibilities at each step, expanding like the branches of a tree.

This method increases the chances of finding a more optimal sequence, much like choosing the best route on a GPS that considers traffic conditions instead of just directing you along the shortest path.

Another pivotal enhancement is the integration of attention layers, which allow the model to focus on different parts of the input sequence at different times, rather than relying solely on the final context vector. This mechanism is akin to a seasoned chef tasting a dish at various stages of preparation to adjust the seasoning perfectly, rather than just at the end. Attention layers help the model to pay "attention" to the most relevant parts of the input data, thereby improving the quality and relevance of the output.

Scheduled sampling is another technique used to refine these models. It involves changing the training strategy over time: Initially, the model is trained mostly with correct outputs, but gradually, it starts receiving its previous predictions as inputs during training. This method helps make the model robust to its own errors, akin to a student learning to catch their own mistakes in a complex calculation.

Real-World Applications: Seeing Sequence-to-Sequence in Action

The practical applications of sequence-to-sequence models are as varied as they are impressive. In the realm of language translation, models like Google Translate help users convert text from one language to another with increasing accuracy. In speech-to-text applications, these models allow for real-time transcription of spoken words into written text, facilitating effective communication for the hearing impaired or in professional settings like courtrooms or corporate meetings.

Moreover, sequence-to-sequence models are making significant inroads in the customer service industry through their deployment in chatbots. These AI-powered bots can handle a range of queries, from simple

FAQs to complex requests, by understanding and generating human-like responses. This not only enhances customer experience but also streamlines operations by handling numerous customer interactions simultaneously, without fatigue or errors.

As we continue to explore and expand the capabilities of sequence-to-sequence models, their role in bridging the human-machine communication gap becomes increasingly evident. Beyond serving as tools for automation, they are pivotal in enhancing interactions and understanding, making machines better equipped to handle the complexities of human language and thought. The evolution of these models is a testament to the remarkable advances in AI, promising even more sophisticated and intuitive applications in the future. As these technologies progress, they continue to transform the landscape of communication and interaction, paving the way for more seamless, efficient, and accurate exchanges in various domains of human activity.

2.5 Utilizing Conditional Generative Models

Step into the world of conditional generative models, where the magic of AI meets the precision of conditions. Unlike their unconditional counterparts, which generate outputs based purely on learned data distributions without specific guidance, conditional models are the savvy artists who don't start painting on a canvas without knowing what's expected. Think of them as commissioned artists who tailor their creations according to the desires of their patrons, be it generating a night sky or a bustling cityscape based on specified inputs.

These models thrive on directives. They can be trained to produce data that isn't just random but perfectly aligned with given conditions or labels. This could mean generating images of dogs when "dog" is specified or crafting sentences in French when tasked with text generation under the condition of "French language". This specificity allows for a more controlled and relevant output, making these models incredibly useful for tasks where customization is key.

Diving deeper, let's talk about some stars of the conditional generation stage: conditional generative adversarial networks (conditional GANs) and conditional variational autoencoders (CVAEs). Conditional GANs extend the basic framework of traditional GANs by incorporating label information into the generation process. This twist allows the generator to produce content that's both high-quality and class specific. For example, in a conditional GAN setup for image generation, feeding a label like "sunset" can direct the generator to produce images that predominantly feature the warm hues and gradients typical of sunsets.

CVAes, on the other hand, bring a flavor of probability to the mix. They are designed to handle uncertainty in inputs by learning to encode input data into a distribution instead of a fixed vector. Each generated output, therefore, considers possible variations, making CVAEs excellent for tasks where variation within a condition is desired. For instance, when generating human faces under the condition of "smiling", a CVAE can produce a variety of smiling faces, each with subtle differences in expressions, reflecting a more lifelike variation.

Practical Magic: Applications of Conditional Generative Models

The applications of these controlled creative geniuses are vast and varied. In personalized content creation, for instance, e-commerce platforms can use these models to generate custom fashion items that align with individual style preferences. By conditioning the model on a user's past behavior or explicitly stated preferences, the system can design personalized product images that are more likely to engage and attract the user.

In digital marketing, the ability to tailor and tweak promotional imagery or content based on specific demographic or psychographic data can enhance engagement rates significantly. A conditional GAN could be used to automatically generate advertising content that resonates with different audiences, adjusting elements like background setting, featured products, and even the models used based on the targeted demographic segments.

Another exciting application lies in targeted data augmentation, especially in the field of medical imaging. Here, conditional models can generate realistic, varied medical images under specific conditions, such as types of diseases or abnormalities. These images can then be used to train diagnostic models, ensuring that they are robust and accurate across a more diverse set of medical scenarios than what limited real-world data might allow.

Navigating the Challenges: Mode Collapse and Beyond

Despite their prowess, training conditional generative models isn't a walk in the park. A notorious challenge is mode collapse, which occurs when the model starts producing limited varieties of outputs, or even the same output repeatedly, despite varying input conditions. This can severely limit the usefulness of the model in practical applications where diversity in output is crucial.

One potential solution is introducing regularization techniques during training that encourage diversity in the generated outputs. Techniques like minibatch discrimination or feature matching can be employed to ensure that the model maintains variability in its outputs, respecting the input conditions without collapsing into sameness.

Another approach is to enhance the model architecture itself. For instance, incorporating feedback loops within the training process, where the diversity of outputs is continually assessed and fed back into the model for adjustments, can help in maintaining the balance between adherence to conditions and output diversity.

Navigating these challenges requires a blend of technical acumen and creative problem-solving, characteristics that are quintessential to the field of AI. As we advance, the sophistication of conditional generative models continues to grow, promising more controlled and relevant outputs and also opening up new horizons where the only limit is the condition you can conceive. Whether it's creating personalized experiences, enhancing training datasets, or generating novel content, these models stand at the ready, poised to transform possibilities into realities in the most conditioned manner imaginable.

2.6 Advanced Techniques in Neural Style Transfer

Let's paint a picture—literally. Imagine you could merge Van Gogh's starry swirls with your favorite selfie, or splash Monet's water lilies onto your latest landscape photo. Welcome to the world of neural style transfer, where the alchemy of AI meets the time-honored craft of artistry. This technique is not just about copying; it's about reinvention. It blends the content of one image with the style of another, transforming standard photos into extraordinary pieces of art.

Neural style transfer uses convolutional neural networks (CNNs) to separate and recombine the content and style of digital images. Here's how it typically works: The "content" image (say, a photograph of a cityscape) and the "style" image (perhaps a famous painting) are fed into the network. The network then analyzes the content image to capture its underlying content and structure, while simultaneously capturing the stylistic features of the style image. The result? A hybrid image that looks like your cityscape painted by the artistic hand of the chosen style.

Algorithmic Improvements: Elevating the Art

As with any good technology, the devil is in the details—or in this case, the algorithms. Innovations like adaptive instance normalization have taken style transfer to new heights. This technique adjusts the mean and variance of the content image to match that of the style image, allowing for faster and more flexible style integration. It's akin to an audio equalizer balancing different sound components to achieve perfect pitch but for visual elements.

Deep photo style transfer is another notable advancement. Traditional methods sometimes struggle with preserving the photorealism of the content image, making the results look more like a painting than a photo. Deep photo style transfer algorithms address this by maintaining the naturalistic elements and realistic details of the content image, ensuring that the final product retains a lifelike quality. This method provides a more seamless blend, where the style is infused subtly without overwhelming the original content's integrity.

Expanding the Canvas: Style Transfer Across Media

Moving beyond static images, style transfer is making waves in video and interactive media, vastly broadening its applications. In video, style transfer can be used to apply artistic effects frame by frame, creating stunning visuals that look as though they've been hand-painted. However, consistency across frames can be a challenge, potentially resulting in a jarring visual experience. Advances in temporal consistency algorithms have begun to tackle this issue, ensuring that the artistic style flows smoothly from one frame to the next, much like maintaining narrative consistency in a film.

Interactive media, including video games and VR, also benefit from real-time style transfer. Imagine playing a game where the environments adapt stylistically to the narrative mood or enjoying a VR experience that can transform your surroundings into the style of different art periods. These applications enhance user engagement and also open new avenues for creative expression within digital environments.

A Renaissance in Creative Industries

The ripple effects of neural style transfer in creative industries like graphic design, fashion, and advertising are profound. Designers can prototype ideas in various artistic styles quickly without manually recreating each style, enhancing creativity and productivity. In fashion, designers experiment with patterns and textures derived from iconic artworks, breathing new life into fabric designs.

Advertising has tapped into style transfer to create visually captivating campaigns that blend brand content with artistic styles, attracting more eyeballs and engaging consumers on a deeper level. This melding of art and commerce stands out in a crowded market as it adds a layer of sophistication and cultural relevance to marketing efforts.

In essence, neural style transfer is not just a technical achievement; it's a tool of transformation. It's reshaping how we interact with and appreciate digital media, turning everyday images into works of art and redefining the boundaries between technology and creativity. As we continue to explore and refine this technology, its potential to revolutionize visual media and open up new realms of artistic possibility continues to grow. The fusion of AI with traditional artistic techniques is more than a novelty—it's a burgeoning field that promises to influence a myriad of industries, pushing the envelope of what's possible in both art and technology.

As this chapter closes, we've journeyed through the interplay of pixels and paintbrushes that neural style transfer embodies. From revitalizing personal photos to transforming industry practices, the blend of technology and art is crafting a future where creativity knows no bounds. Looking ahead, the next chapter will delve into another fascinating aspect of generative AI, opening up new vistas of knowledge and application. Stay tuned, as the adventure is just getting more intriguing.

PRACTICAL APPLICATIONS OF **GENERATIVE AI**

Image Generation

Predictive Analytics

Content Creation

Virtual Worlds

Art and Design

Chapter 3:

Practical Applications of Generative AI

Welcome to the digital renaissance, an era where generative AI is not just a participant but a frontrunner in the creative sphere. This chapter isn't just about understanding generative AI; it's about seeing it in action, transforming how we create and consume content across various mediums. Brace yourself as we dive into the vibrant world of digital media, where AI isn't just a tool but a collaborator, ready to co-create everything from blockbuster movie edits to personalized streaming playlists that seem to read your mood.

3.1 Generative AI in Content Creation: Text, Images, and Video

Revolutionizing Digital Media Production

Imagine, if you will, a world where tedious video editing tasks are handled by AI, leaving directors and editors free to focus on the creative aspects of filmmaking. Generative AI is making this a reality. Automatic video editing tools powered by AI can trim scenes, adjust sound levels, and even suggest the best clips to capture the viewer's attention. Similarly, image enhancement techniques through AI are nothing short of wizardry. A blurry, old photo can be restored to a crisp image, with every smile and sunset brought back to vivid life. These tools analyze the data behind the pixels, enhancing quality without losing the essence of the original—think of it as digital Botox for photographs.

Personalizing Content: A New Frontier

The magic of generative AI extends into the realm of personalization, transforming how content is tailored to individual preferences. In the entertainment industry, this technology is like a personal DJ or a film curator who knows exactly what you want to watch or listen to before you do. By analyzing your previous interactions, AI can predict what might catch your fancy, be it a jazz album or a sci-fi movie. This isn't just about keeping audiences engaged; by creating a unique connection with each user, every digital experience feels like it was crafted just for them.

The Art of AI-Driven Text Generation

Now, let's talk about text. Generative AI is becoming quite the wordsmith, thanks to advancements in natural language processing. From whipping up articles about the latest tech trends to penning a romantic novel, AI-driven text generation is here to stay. Tools like automated journalism are already being used by major news outlets to create content on topics as diverse as sports and finance. These systems are trained on vast datasets to produce articles that are informative, well-structured, and remarkably human-like. The technology behind this involves models that understand context and can generate coherent narratives, ensuring that the text is not just grammatically correct but also engaging.

Redefining Graphic Design

In the visually driven world of graphic design, AI is playing an increasingly creative role. Imagine an AI that can generate dozens of logo designs or page layouts in seconds. These systems use parameters set by designers—such as color schemes, typography, and style preferences—to create multiple iterations for specific projects. This not only speeds up the design process but also offers designers a variety of options to refine and amalgamate. It's like having a brainstorming session with a non-human colleague who doesn't need coffee breaks.

Visual Element: Infographic on AI in Film Production

How AI Transforms Film Editing and Production:

1. **Scene Selection:** AI algorithms analyze hours of footage to select key scenes based on cinematic techniques and narrative significance.

2. **Color Grading:** AI tools automatically adjust colors to enhance visual consistency and mood throughout the film.

3. **Sound Optimization:** AI enhances audio quality by balancing levels, removing background noise, and synchronizing audio with visuals.

4. **Special Effects:** AI streamlines the creation of visual effects, from background enhancements to complex character animations.

5. **Audience Engagement:** AI predicts audience preferences to suggest changes that might increase viewer engagement and satisfaction.

This infographic serves as a snapshot of how AI is not just an addition but a transformational force in the film industry, streamlining processes and enhancing creative outputs. As we continue to explore the depths of generative AI's capabilities in content creation, it becomes clear that the line between creator and creation is blurring. AI is no longer just a tool; it's a partner in the creative process, offering both efficiency and inspiration. As we forge ahead, the potential for new and innovative applications of generative AI in digital media is boundless, promising exciting developments that will continue to revolutionize how we create, consume, and interact with content.

Test your creativity with Runway ML's image-to-video generator:

3.2 Implementing AI in Web Development and Design

In the digital playground where web developers and designers spend their days (and often nights), artificial intelligence is swiftly moving from a handy tool to an essential co-worker. Imagine a world where the tedious nuances of web design, from crafting the perfect color palette to laying out pages, are intelligently automated. This isn't the stuff of science fiction; it's happening now, reshaping the landscape of web development and design with each passing algorithm.

Automating the Art of Web Design

The process begins with AI's role in streamlining web design, particularly through automating repetitive and time-consuming tasks. Tools powered by AI can now analyze brand assets and user interfaces to suggest or even directly implement design elements. This includes everything from choosing a color scheme that complies with accessibility standards to laying out elements in a way that maximizes user engagement. For instance, based on the target audience's preferences and past interaction data, AI can suggest adjustments to a site's design that might better capture attention or encourage clicks. This isn't just about making sites look pretty; it's about crafting user experiences that are both aesthetically pleasing and functionally optimal.

Imagine the scenario where a fledgling online store wants to establish a unique identity. An AI-driven design tool can quickly generate several website templates that not only match the brand's color scheme but also organize content in a way that highlights featured products. This capability isn't just efficient; it democratizes design, allowing smaller players to compete with established giants without the need for hefty budgets.

Creating More Dynamic Interactions

Moving deeper into the realm of user interaction, AI's ability to enhance the dynamism of web elements is nothing short of revolutionary. Consider AI-generated animations that respond to user interactions in real time or dynamic interfaces that adapt based on the user's behavior. For example, a learning platform can use AI to change its interface based on the time of day, reducing eye strain with darker colors in the evening or keeping things bright and engaging during the day.

This adaptability extends to how information is presented. AI can analyze user engagement metrics to optimize the display of content, ensuring that users see what they are most likely to be interested in, without overwhelming them with choices. This kind of intelligent responsiveness not only makes for smoother user experiences but also helps in building interfaces that are deeply personalized, making each interaction feel like it's tailored specifically to the user.

Optimizing User Experience Through Behavioral Insights

The magic of AI in enhancing user experience lies in its ability to sift through and make sense of vast amounts of data on user behavior. By understanding how users interact with a site, AI can help create more intuitive layouts and navigation paths. Tools like heatmaps and session replays are processed by AI to give designers precise insights into which parts of a website attract the most attention and where users most frequently disengage.

From these insights, AI can suggest modifications to the website structure or content placement that enhance navigability and retain user interest longer. For instance, if an e-commerce site finds that users often leave the checkout page before completing a purchase, AI can help redesign that page to make it more straightforward or more reassuring, perhaps by simplifying the information required or by adding clearer security badges.

Streamlining Development Workflows

On the back end, AI significantly streamlines the development workflow, making the life of a web developer less about debugging endless lines of code and more about strategic thinking and creative problem-solving. AI-powered tools can now assist in writing code by suggesting completions or corrections, much like a copilot in the cockpit of a plane. This not only speeds up the development process but also reduces errors, ensuring higher quality and consistency across web projects.

Moreover, AI's capability to detect potential bugs or inefficiencies in code before it goes live is a game-changer. It's like having a seasoned mentor looking over your shoulder, ready to point out a misstep before it turns into a stumble. This proactive problem-solving saves countless hours that would otherwise be spent in testing and troubleshooting, allowing teams to focus on more strategic tasks such as enhancing user engagement or integrating innovative features.

As we navigate through this chapter, it becomes clear that AI's integration into web development and design reshapes these fields and sets a new standard for what's possible. From automating design tasks to optimizing user interactions and streamlining development workflows, AI is at the forefront, driving innovations that deliver more personalized, engaging, and efficient web experiences. This evolution is not just about keeping up with the times; it's about setting the pace, ensuring that web platforms are functional, beautiful, smart, adaptive, and ready to meet the ever-changing demands of the digital age. For developers and designers, embracing these AI-driven tools and techniques isn't just beneficial; it's imperative for staying relevant and competitive in a world where web experiences are constantly redefined by technology.

3.3 AI-Driven Solutions for E-commerce and Retail

In the bustling world of e-commerce and retail, AI is a game changer, reshaping the landscape from the ground up. Imagine walking into a store where the shelves rearrange themselves to display products tailored specifically to your tastes and needs or an online shop that knows your style better than you do. This scenario isn't far-fetched; it's the current reality in spaces where AI-driven solutions are employed to personalize shopping experiences, streamline inventory management, enhance virtual try-ons, and revolutionize customer service.

Tailoring the Shopping Experience to Individual Tastes

Personalization is the secret sauce in today's retail environment, and AI is the chef. By analyzing data from user interactions such as past purchases, search history, and even page views, AI algorithms can predict what products a customer might be interested in next. This doesn't bombard shoppers with random suggestions; it creates a curated experience that feels personal and relevant. For instance, if you've been browsing outdoor gear, AI might highlight the latest eco-friendly hiking boots or a high-tech tent that's just hit the market, enhancing your engagement and encouraging purchases.

The sophistication of AI in understanding individual preferences can be seen in how promotions are tailored. Special offers, discounts, and even product bundles are customized to meet the anticipated needs and desires of each shopper. For example, an AI system might notice that you frequently buy ingredients for baking, so it suggests a bundle offer on a new mixer, premium flour, and artisanal vanilla extract, all at a discounted price. This level of customization not only improves customer satisfaction but also increases the likelihood of upselling and cross-selling, significantly boosting retail sales.

Streamlining Inventory With Smart Forecasting

On the flip side of the consumer experience is inventory management—a critical, albeit less glamorous, aspect of retail. AI dramatically transforms this arena through precise demand forecasting and stock optimization. By analyzing patterns in sales data, seasonality, and market trends, AI can predict future product demand with high accuracy. This predictive power allows retailers to optimize their stock levels, ensuring they have enough products to meet customer demand, and simultaneously avoid overstocking, which can tie up capital and increase storage costs.

Imagine the AI systems at work before a major holiday sale, analyzing years of data to predict which products will be in high demand. This information helps retailers prepare their inventory accordingly, reducing the risk of stockouts and excess inventory. Furthermore, AI can dynamically adjust these predictions based on real-time sales data, reacting to unexpected changes in demand or supply chain disruptions.

This agility in inventory management not only reduces waste but also ensures that businesses can operate more sustainably.

Revolutionizing Online Fitting Rooms with Virtual Try-Ons

Virtual try-ons represent another fascinating application of AI in retail, bridging the gap between online shopping and the in-store experience. Using AI algorithms, customers can see how clothes will look on them through their digital devices, without ever having to step into a store. This technology uses a combination of computer vision, machine learning, and augmented reality to analyze the user's body dimensions and the way different fabrics and styles drape on their figure.

This isn't just a cool gadget; it's a practical solution that addresses one of the biggest pain points in online apparel shopping: uncertainty about fit and appearance. Virtual try-ons can dramatically reduce this uncertainty, boosting consumer confidence in online purchases. The result? Happier customers and fewer returns. For retailers, this means lower logistics costs and a better bottom line, not to mention a more sustainable operation with fewer items being returned and shipped back and forth.

Enhancing Customer Service with AI-driven Interactions

Lastly, let's turn our attention to customer service, where AI is making significant inroads. AI chatbots and virtual assistants are now commonplace in handling customer inquiries and service requests. These AI systems are designed to understand and process natural language, allowing them to interact with customers in a way that feels both personal and efficient. Whether it's answering FAQs, processing returns, or tracking order statuses, AI can handle a multitude of customer service tasks without breaking a sweat.

But AI's role in customer service goes beyond mere conversation handling. It can analyze customer sentiment, adjust its responses accordingly, and even escalate issues to human agents when necessary. This seamless integration of AI and human service ensures that customers receive quick, empathetic, and effective support. In an era where customer experience can make or break a business, AI-driven customer service is no longer just an option; it's a necessity.

As we navigate through these applications, it becomes evident that AI is changing the retail landscape by setting a new standard for how businesses operate and engage with their customers. From personalized shopping experiences to efficient inventory management, and from innovative virtual try-ons to enhanced customer service, AI is at the heart of modern retail innovation. For businesses, embracing these AI-driven solutions isn't just about staying competitive; it's about leading in a world where technology and customer expectations are ever-evolving.

3.4 Enhancing User Experience with AI Chatbots

In the bustling digital marketplace, where the currency is convenience and the language is speed, AI chatbots are the diligent, multitasking shop assistants of the future. Gone are the days of waiting on hold to the tune of elevator music, only to be greeted by a harried customer service agent. Today, AI chatbots are revolutionizing customer interactions with their ability to handle queries, provide information, and resolve issues—all without breaking a sweat or, more aptly, without human intervention. But how do these digital wizards manage to keep customers satisfied and engaged? Let's peel back the curtain on this technological marvel.

AI chatbots are designed to simulate human conversation, but their capabilities extend far beyond simple scripted responses. They employ sophisticated algorithms to understand and process user requests, whether it's a question about a product, a complaint, or a request for assistance. Imagine a customer inquiring about a laptop's specifications on an online store. The AI chatbot can instantly pull up the relevant information, provide detailed responses, and even suggest additional products based on the customer's interests. This instantaneous, 24/7 response system not only enhances customer satisfaction but also streamlines the resolution process, allowing issues to be handled swiftly and efficiently.

But the prowess of AI chatbots isn't confined to mere transactional interactions. They excel in personalizing communications, making each conversation as unique as the customer. By analyzing past interactions, purchase history, and even browsing patterns, AI chatbots can tailor their dialogue to match the customer's preferences and history. This personalized approach not only makes interactions more engaging but also builds a rapport with customers, akin to a favorite store clerk who remembers your taste and recommends products accordingly. This level of personalization ensures that customers are not just heard but also understood, fostering loyalty and enhancing the overall customer experience.

Crossing language barriers, AI chatbots also bring multilingual support to the table, allowing businesses to expand their reach and cater to a global audience. With the ability to converse in multiple languages, these chatbots can serve customers from different linguistic backgrounds without the need for extensive human intervention. Whether it's responding to a customer in Spanish, French, or Mandarin, AI chatbots can manage conversations with the same ease and accuracy, broadening the customer base and enhancing accessibility. This multilingual capability is particularly beneficial in today's globalized market, where businesses strive to create inclusive and diverse customer experiences that resonate across cultural and linguistic boundaries.

Furthermore, AI chatbots excel in automating routine tasks that, while necessary, can be monotonous and time-consuming. From scheduling appointments to tracking orders, these tasks are handled with precision and efficiency by AI systems. Consider a scenario where a customer needs to book a warranty service for a gadget. An AI chatbot can handle the entire process—from checking warranty eligibility and understanding the issue to scheduling an appointment with a service technician. By automating these tasks, AI chatbots free up human agents to tackle more complex issues while also ensuring that these routine tasks are performed flawlessly with reduced errors and enhanced efficiency.

As we explore the multifaceted roles of AI chatbots in enhancing customer interactions, it becomes clear that they are not just functional tools but strategic assets in improving customer service. Their ability to provide quick, personalized, and accurate responses transforms the customer service landscape, setting new standards in customer engagement and satisfaction. In an era where the customer experience can significantly influence business success, AI chatbots stand out as essential elements in crafting interactions that are not only efficient but also genuinely satisfying. As businesses continue to harness the power of AI, the evolution of chatbots will likely continue, bringing even more sophisticated and intuitive interactions that could redefine customer service in ways we are just beginning to imagine.

3.5 Generative Models in Healthcare: Opportunities and Challenges

In the vast and complex world of healthcare, where decisions can have life-altering implications, generative AI is emerging as a transformative force. Imagine a scenario where the accuracy of medical diagnoses surges forward, leaving behind the constraints and errors of traditional methods. Generative AI models enhance the precision and speed of diagnostics, particularly in medical imaging. These advanced algorithms can interpret complex imaging data, such as MRIs and CT scans, with a level of detail and accuracy that surpasses human capabilities. By training on vast datasets of medical images, these AI systems learn to detect subtle patterns and anomalies that might escape even the most trained eyes. For instance, in the detection of early-stage cancer, AI models can identify minute signs of tumor formations that are often critical for early intervention and successful treatment outcomes.

The power of generative AI extends beyond diagnostics into the realm of personalized medicine. Each patient's journey through illness and treatment is unique, influenced by their genetic makeup, lifestyle, and even their environment. AI models excel in sifting through this complex web of data to recommend personalized treatment plans. By analyzing a patient's medical history, genetic information, and current health status, AI systems can tailor treatment strategies that optimize effectiveness while minimizing side effects. This is not about replacing doctors but empowering them with tools that can make more informed decisions, backed by data-driven insights. For example, in the treatment of chronic diseases such as diabetes, AI can help in designing a personalized management plan that adjusts medications and lifestyle interventions based on real-time changes in the patient's condition.

The ability to generate synthetic medical data is another frontier where generative AI is making significant strides. In medical research, the availability of comprehensive and diverse data sets is often a bottleneck, limited by privacy concerns and the rarity of certain conditions. Generative AI models can create realistic, anonymized data sets that mimic the properties of real patient data, providing researchers with the resources needed to conduct robust and extensive studies. This synthetic data generation can accelerate drug development and clinical trials, making it quicker and less costly to bring new treatments to market. Moreover, it ensures that patient privacy is maintained, as the data used no longer ties back to real individuals, thus navigating one of the significant ethical concerns in medical research.

Speaking of ethics, the integration of AI in healthcare is a minefield of ethical considerations that must be navigated with care. The use of AI in diagnosing and treating patients introduces a new level of complexity to the already intricate ethical landscape of healthcare. Issues such as data privacy, the transparency of AI decisions, and the potential for bias in AI models are at the forefront of discussions. For AI to be effectively and ethically integrated into healthcare, it is crucial that these systems are not only accurate and efficient but also transparent and fair. Patients and practitioners must be able to trust AI systems, understanding how decisions are made and ensuring that these decisions are free of bias. Moreover, the regulatory frameworks that govern the use of AI in healthcare must be robust and adaptive, capable of keeping pace with the rapid advancements in AI technology.

As we explore the potential of generative AI in healthcare, it becomes evident that this technology holds the promise to revolutionize medical practice. From enhancing diagnostic accuracy and personalizing treatment plans to generating synthetic data and navigating ethical challenges, AI's role in healthcare is multifaceted and profoundly impactful. As we continue to harness these capabilities, the focus must remain on developing AI systems that are not only technologically advanced but also ethically sound and aligned with the fundamental goal of healthcare—improving patient outcomes and quality of life. The journey of integrating AI into healthcare is complex and challenging, but the potential benefits are immense, promising a future where healthcare is more accurate, personalized, and accessible.

3.6 AI in Financial Modeling and Risk Assessment

In the high-stakes world of finance, fortunes can be made or lost in the blink of an eye. To mitigate these risks, artificial intelligence (AI) is not just a luxury—it's a necessity. Imagine a scenario where AI algorithms sift through mountains of financial data, predicting market trends that are invisible to the human eye. This isn't a scene from a futuristic movie; it's happening right now, as AI reshapes the landscape of financial modeling and risk assessment.

Predicting Market Trends with AI Precision

Financial markets are notoriously difficult to predict, with myriad factors influencing global trends. Enter AI, with its ability to analyze vast datasets quickly and accurately. AI models use historical data and real-time inputs to identify patterns and predict future market movements, giving traders and investors a much-needed edge. By employing techniques like machine learning, these models can adapt and improve their predictions over time, learning from market shifts and behavioral changes. This proactive approach allows financial analysts to make more informed decisions, backed by data-driven insights that traditional methods might miss. Whether it's spotting a potential stock surge or foreseeing a market downturn, AI provides a strategic advantage that is transforming investment strategies across the globe.

Enhancing Risk Management through AI

Risk management is another critical area where AI is making significant inroads. In the world of finance, understanding and mitigating risk is paramount. AI excels in this by providing tools that assess and predict risks with greater precision. For instance, in credit risk assessment, AI algorithms analyze borrower data to predict the likelihood of default. This analysis is based on a range of factors, including credit history, transaction patterns, and even social media behavior. By integrating these diverse data points, AI provides a holistic view of credit risk that is far more nuanced than traditional methods.

Fraud detection is another arena where AI proves indispensable. Financial fraud can manifest in myriad forms, from credit card fraud to complex securities fraud. AI systems are trained to detect anomalies and patterns indicative of fraudulent activity, often catching these signs before a human analyst would. Moreover, AI's ability to continuously learn and adapt makes it particularly effective in staying ahead of sophisticated fraud techniques that evolve rapidly. This preemptive detection is crucial in safeguarding assets and maintaining financial integrity.

Streamlining Trade With Algorithmic Trading

Algorithmic trading, where trades are executed at high speeds by AI systems, is reshaping the trading floors of financial institutions. These AI-driven trading platforms can analyze market conditions in real-time, executing trades at optimal prices that humans simply can't match in speed. The algorithms are designed to monitor market variables continuously and can adjust trading strategies instantaneously. This capability not only maximizes profits but also minimizes losses, especially in volatile market conditions where speed is of the essence. By leveraging AI in algorithmic trading, financial institutions can ensure more efficient and effective trading strategies, which are crucial in a world where milliseconds can mean the difference between profit and loss.

Ensuring Compliance Through AI

Navigating the complex world of financial regulations is a daunting task for any institution. AI comes to the rescue by automating compliance processes, ensuring that financial institutions adhere to laws and regulations efficiently. AI systems can analyze vast amounts of legal documents and transaction records to ensure compliance with regulatory requirements. This analysis includes monitoring transactions for signs of money laundering, ensuring that trading activities comply with securities regulations, and keeping up with the constantly changing landscape of financial laws.

AI not only simplifies compliance but also makes it more accurate, reducing the risk of costly legal penalties for noncompliance. Moreover, as financial regulations continue to evolve, AI systems can adapt quickly, updating their parameters to match new legal frameworks without significant downtime or overhaul.

As we wrap up this exploration of AI's role in financial modeling and risk assessment, it's clear that AI is not just a tool; it's a transformational force that is redefining the financial industry. From predicting market trends and managing risks to automating trading and ensuring regulatory compliance, AI's capabilities are vast, and its potential is immense. As we move forward, embracing these AI-driven innovations will be key to staying competitive and successful in the rapidly evolving world of finance.

Looking ahead, the next chapter will dive into another fascinating application of AI, exploring its role in environmental sustainability. Stay tuned as we uncover how AI is not only powering financial markets but also paving the way for a more sustainable future.

TOOLS AND PLATFORMS FOR GENERATIVE AI

Chapter 4:

Tools and Platforms for Generative AI

Welcome to the digital artist's studio of the 21st century, where the paint is data, and the brushes are sophisticated software tools that can learn, adapt, and create. Here, in this chapter, we're diving into the treasure trove of tools that make generative AI not just a possibility but a dynamic reality. Let's pull back the curtain on TensorFlow, a powerhouse in the AI toolset, guiding you from your first tentative steps to high-speed sprints in the world of generative models.

4.1 Getting Started With TensorFlow for Generative AI

Explore TensorFlow's Ecosystem: A Universe of Possibilities

Imagine stepping into a workshop equipped with every tool you could possibly need—welcome to TensorFlow. This open-source library is not just a tool; it's a sprawling ecosystem designed to push the boundaries of what AI can achieve. At the heart of this ecosystem are TensorFlow Graphics and TensorFlow Probability, two of the jewels in TensorFlow's crown that specifically shine in the realm of generative AI.

TensorFlow Graphics offers a suite of tools and libraries that integrate seamlessly with TensorFlow to handle complex, data-driven visualizations and 3D model generations. Whether you're sculpting the features of a new video game character or simulating intricate weather patterns, TensorFlow Graphics ensures that your models aren't just smart but visually stunning.

On the flip side, TensorFlow Probability deals with the uncertainties of the real world, providing a statistical foundation for your models. This library allows you to inject a dose of probability into your AI, handling everything from random number generation to sophisticated statistical models that can predict, learn, and infer with an understanding of the chaos inherent in the real world.

Hands-on with TensorFlow: Building Your First Generative Model

Now, let's roll up our sleeves and get our hands dirty. Building your first generative model with TensorFlow is like assembling your first robot kit—thrilling, a bit daunting, but immensely satisfying. Here's a step-by-step guide to setting up a basic generative adversarial network (GAN):

1. **Environment Setup:** Start by installing TensorFlow. Ensure you have the right pip package installed in your Python environment.

2. **Define the Model:** Use the TensorFlow Keras API to define two models—the Generator and the Discriminator. The Generator creates new data instances, while the Discriminator evaluates them.

3. **Set the Loss Functions:** These functions will help train your models. Typically, cross-entropy loss functions are used to gauge how well the Generator's outputs trick the Discriminator.

4. **Training and Backpropagation:** Employ TensorFlow's optimizing functions to minimize loss, adjusting your model parameters to improve both the Generator and Discriminator.

The beauty of TensorFlow is in its versatility. The same tools that help you model virtual clouds are also capable of creating digital artwork or simulating complex economic models. As you tinker with your GAN, remember: Every error is a lesson, and every iteration brings you closer to mastery.

Integration Capabilities: TensorFlow in the Tech Ecosystem

TensorFlow is designed to play well with others. Its ability to integrate with various data sources and software platforms enhances its utility for large-scale projects. Whether it's ingesting huge datasets from cloud storage solutions like Google Cloud or collaborating with other AI and machine learning frameworks, TensorFlow is like the friendly neighbor who's ready to lend a hand or a cup of data, so to speak.

For developers looking to scale their AI models to production, TensorFlow's Serving component offers a flexible, high-performance serving system, designed specifically for machine learning models. It handles the practical aspects of deploying models, from versioning to managing APIs, ensuring that your AI creations can smoothly transition from prototypes to functional real-world applications.

Community and Resources: The Human Network Behind TensorFlow

Behind every great tool is an even greater community. TensorFlow's user community is a vibrant network of developers, researchers, and enthusiasts, all driven by a passion for AI innovation. Whether you're stuck debugging your model at 2 a.m. or looking for inspiration for your next project, TensorFlow's forums and user groups are treasure troves of knowledge and support.

Moreover, the internet is awash with tutorials, guides, and courses dedicated to TensorFlow. These resources range from beginner-friendly introductions to advanced deep dives, covering every conceivable aspect of working with TensorFlow. Whether you prefer learning through video tutorials, blog posts, or formal coursework, a wealth of knowledge is just waiting to be tapped into.

As you embark on your journey with TensorFlow, remember that you're becoming part of a global community. This community doesn't just use TensorFlow—they shape its future by contributing to its code, sharing innovative uses, and supporting one another through challenges. This collaborative spirit drives TensorFlow forward, ensuring that it remains at the cutting edge of AI technology, ready to meet the needs of tomorrow's challenges.

So, grab your digital paintbrush and let TensorFlow be your guide. Whether you're crafting detailed 3D models, simulating complex systems, or generating new data that mimics the real world, TensorFlow offers the tools, the support, and the community to help you succeed. Dive in, experiment, and let your creative juices flow—the canvas of generative AI awaits.

4.2 Mastering PyTorch for Advanced AI Development

Advanced Features of PyTorch: Empowering AI Exploration

Let's explore the realm of PyTorch, where the boundaries of AI are not just pushed but often completely redefined. PyTorch shines with its dynamic computation graphs, a feature that stands out for its adaptability during the model's runtime. Unlike static graphs, which define a blueprint that cannot be altered once execution starts, PyTorch's dynamic graphs evolve as they execute. This allows you to change the behavior of your model on the fly, depending on the inputs it receives, which is akin to a GPS system recalculating your route when you decide to make an unexpected detour.

Another jewel in PyTorch's crown is its native support for advanced automatic differentiation operations (autograd). Autograd automates the calculation of forward and backward passes in neural networks, which is essential for training deep learning models. This feature saves time and ensures that the gradients are computed accurately, a crucial aspect when you're working on complex models where the slightest error can throw your results off balance.

Implementing Complex Models: A Step-by-Step Exploration

Let's roll up our digital sleeves and get coding with PyTorch. Imagine you're crafting a sophisticated piece of AI art, and at this moment, you're choosing which colors and brushes you need. In AI terms, that translates to selecting the architecture of your model. For this exercise, let's focus on building a variational autoencoder (VAE). Here's how you could start:

1. **Define the Architecture:** Set up the encoder and decoder. The encoder compresses the input into a latent space, and the decoder reconstructs the input from this compressed representation.

2. **Specify the Loss Function:** For a VAE, you typically use a combination of a reconstruction loss (like MSE) and a KL divergence loss, which helps in regularizing the encoder by comparing the distribution of the encoded data to a prior distribution.

3. **Optimizer and Backpropagation:** Initialize an optimizer (such as Adam) and use it to minimize the loss. PyTorch's autograd makes this step straightforward by automatically calculating the gradients.

4. **Training Loop:** Set up your training loop, feeding batches of data to the model, calculating the loss, and updating the model parameters. PyTorch's dynamic computation graph allows modifications on-the-go,

making it easier to tweak your model during training based on specific conditions.

This hands-on approach not only solidifies your understanding of PyTorch's operations but also empowers you to experiment with more complex models, such as conditional GANs, which you can use to manipulate the generative process based on certain conditions to produce customized outputs.

Explore TensorFlow:

PyTorch in Academia and Industry: A Versatile Tool

PyTorch's flexibility and ease of use have made it a favorite among academics for research and experimentation. Its intuitive design and extensive documentation allow researchers to quickly prototype and iterate on their ideas, which is invaluable in the fast-paced world of academic research. In industry, PyTorch is equally revered, utilized in diverse sectors from automotive to finance for developing commercial AI applications. Companies appreciate PyTorch for its robustness and scalability, which enable the deployment of complex AI models into production environments.

Ecosystem and Extensions: Expanding PyTorch's Functionality

Beyond its core capabilities, PyTorch is supported by an extensive ecosystem of tools and libraries that enhance its functionality. TorchText and TorchVision are two such libraries that extend PyTorch's capabilities to perform natural language processing and computer vision. TorchText simplifies the preprocessing of textual data, providing support for common tasks such as tokenization and batch generation, which are essential for training language models. TorchVision, on the other hand, comes loaded with pretrained models like VGG and ResNet and tools for image transformations, making it incredibly easy to implement state-of-the-art computer vision algorithms.

Whether you're a novice just stepping into the world of AI or a seasoned professional looking to deepen your expertise, PyTorch offers the tools, flexibility, and community support to take your projects from conception to completion. Dive in, explore, and let PyTorch guide you through the thrilling landscape of artificial intelligence development.

Explore PyTorch:

4.3 Leveraging OpenAI's GPT for Custom Uses

Overview of GPT Models: A Trek Through AI's Evolution

Let's take a stroll down the memory lane of AI development, focusing on OpenAI's GPT (generative pre-trained transformer) series from its initial iteration, GPT-1, through to the more sophisticated GPT-3. These models have not just grown in size but in intellect, akin to watching a child prodigy evolve into a polymath. The core of these models lies in their transformer architecture, which fundamentally changes how machines understand and generate human language. Unlike traditional models that process words in sequence, GPT models handle multiple words simultaneously, capturing nuances of language that were previously elusive.

GPT-3, the latest in the lineup, is a behemoth in terms of size and capability, boasting an astonishing 175 billion parameters. This allows it to generate text that can be eerily human-like, capable of composing poetry, drafting legal documents, and even crafting technical articles that could pass off as written by expert human hands. The evolution from GPT-1 to GPT-3 involves significant improvements in scale and the model's increasing ability to understand context and generate responses that are contextually appropriate, making it an invaluable tool for a range of applications from automated customer service to creative content generation.

Custom Applications of GPT: Tailoring AI to Fit Your Needs

Imagine having a digital assistant that responds to queries while also anticipating needs and personalizing interactions. GPT models are perfect for this role, especially in creating personalized chatbots. These AI-driven chatbots can handle a range of tasks from answering customer inquiries to providing personalized shopping advice, and their ability to learn from interactions means that they get better over time. But that's just scratching the surface.

In content generation, GPT's capabilities can be directed to produce everything from novel content for blogs to scripts for video games. The key here is customization; by fine-tuning the model on specific genres or styles, GPT can produce content that resonates with the intended audience, maintaining a consistent voice that reflects the brand's identity or the user's creative vision. For instance, a travel blog can utilize GPT to generate destination guides that not only provide useful information but do so in an engaging, conversational tone that enhances the reader's experience.

Accessing GPT via API: Connecting to a Powerhouse of Creativity

Harnessing the power of GPT models is made seamless through OpenAI's API, which provides a gateway to integrating this powerful AI into your applications. The process begins with setting up an account with OpenAI and obtaining API keys—a simple yet crucial step that grants you access to a suite of AI functions. Using these APIs involves sending JSON formatted text to the API endpoints, where the heavy lifting of generating responses is done by the GPT model hosted on OpenAI's servers.

For developers, this means that incorporating state-of-the-art language processing capabilities into your app doesn't require colossal infrastructure or deep expertise in machine learning. Instead, you can focus on designing user experiences and crafting the logic to integrate AI-generated content or responses. The API also supports different configurations and fine-tuning options, allowing you to control aspects like response length, style, and even the specificity of information, tailoring the output to meet your specific needs.

Ethical Considerations and Limitations: Navigating the AI Landscape Responsibly

As with any powerful tool, the use of GPT models comes with great responsibility. One of the pressing concerns is the potential for generating misleading or biased content. Since GPT models learn from vast swaths of internet text, they can inadvertently learn and perpetuate biases present in the training data. It's crucial, therefore, to implement safeguards that monitor and mitigate such biases. This might involve setting filters for sensitive topics or manually reviewing generated content before publication.

Another ethical consideration is the transparency of AI-generated content. In an era where misinformation can spread rapidly, it's vital to ensure that content generated by AI is clearly labeled so users can distinguish between human and machine-generated text. This transparency not only fosters trust but also encourages critical engagement with content, ensuring that AI remains a tool for enhancing human creativity and productivity, rather than a source of deception.

Navigating these ethical waters is essential for anyone looking to leverage GPT in their operations. By approaching AI with a mindset that prioritizes ethical considerations and strives for fairness and transparency, developers and businesses can harness the capabilities of GPT models while maintaining ethical integrity and trust.

4.4 Exploring Google's Vertex AI Capabilities

Capabilities of Vertex AI: A Symphony of AI Tools

Imagine stepping into a control room where every lever and button is fine-tuned to manage and enhance your AI projects. This is the essence of Google's Vertex AI: a suite engineered to transform the way we approach machine learning tasks. At the heart of Vertex AI lies its crown jewel, AutoML, a tool that democratizes machine learning by automating the creation of models. Even if you're not a seasoned data scientist, AutoML allows you to develop models tailored to your data, simplifying what was once a complex process.

Then there's AI Platform Pipelines, which introduces a structured canvas to deploy and manage machine learning workflows. Think of it as setting up a manufacturing line for your AI projects, ensuring that each component, from data ingestion to model training, is seamlessly connected and maintained. This tool is particularly crucial when handling sophisticated projects that require robust, repeatable processes.

Not stopping there, Vertex AI also offers Model Monitoring—a vigilant watchdog for your AI models. It keeps an eye on model performance, alerts you of any degradation, and provides recommendations for recalibration. This feature is indispensable, especially in dynamic environments where data and conditions constantly evolve, ensuring that your models adapt and continue to perform optimally.

Integrating Vertex AI Into Workflows: Real-World Alchemy

To truly appreciate the versatility of Vertex AI, let's delve into some real-world applications. Consider a retail company aiming to enhance its customer recommendation system. By integrating Vertex AI, the company can utilize AutoML to refine its recommendation algorithms, ensuring that customers receive personalized product suggestions. Vertex AI's seamless integration into existing workflows means that the company can continue to use its current data management systems while Vertex AI enhances their capabilities, turning routine recommendations into personalized shopping experiences.

Another case study involves a healthcare provider using AI Platform Pipelines to manage patient data more effectively. By creating a workflow that includes data preprocessing, analysis, and predictive modeling, the provider can identify at-risk patients earlier and intervene more effectively. Vertex AI streamlines these processes and ensures they are repeatable and scalable, accommodating an increasing influx of data without loss of performance.

Scalability and Management: Growing With Grace

As your AI endeavors expand, so does the complexity of managing them. Vertex AI excels in scaling, not just in terms of handling larger datasets or more complex models but also in its ability to maintain efficiency and manage resources. Whether it's deploying models across multiple environments or managing various versions of a model, Vertex AI provides tools that make these tasks manageable.

For instance, consider an e-commerce platform experiencing rapid growth. As the number of users increases, so does the variety and volume of data. Vertex AI helps scale the company's predictive models to handle this growth, ensuring that recommendations remain accurate and relevant, even as the underlying data changes rapidly. This scalability is crucial for businesses that cannot afford downtime or sluggish performance, as it ensures that AI systems grow in capability without compromising speed or accuracy.

Security and Compliance: The Shield of Modern AI

In an era where data breaches are all too common, security is both a necessity and a mandate. Vertex AI is built with security at its core, employing robust encryption methods to protect data at rest and in transit. This means that whether your data is stored in the cloud or being processed, it is shielded from unauthorized access.

Furthermore, compliance is a critical aspect, especially for industries like healthcare and finance, where regulations dictate how data should be handled. Vertex AI adheres to international data protection regulations, such as GDPR and HIPAA, ensuring that your AI solutions are not just powerful but also in line with global standards. This compliance is supported by comprehensive audit trails and governance tools that allow you to monitor and control access to your AI systems, ensuring that they are used responsibly and ethically.

As you harness the capabilities of Vertex AI, you're accessing a powerful tool that will ensure that your AI projects are efficient, scalable, secure, and compliant. This suite of features doesn't just support your current needs but also anticipates future challenges, preparing you to face them with confidence. Whether you're a startup looking to innovate or an established enterprise aiming to optimize, Vertex AI equips you with the tools to transform your AI aspirations into tangible successes.

Explore Google Vertex:

4.5 Utilizing Hugging Face for Model Training and Deployment

Step into the bustling digital agora that is Hugging Face, where the exchange of ideas, models, and cutting-edge AI research happens faster than a New York minute. Hugging Face is not just a platform; it's a thriving community where the democratization of AI tools and models takes center stage. With its flagship libraries like Transformers and Datasets, Hugging Face simplifies the deployment of state-of-the-art models, making advanced AI technologies accessible to developers across the globe, regardless of whether they're tinkering in a garage or strategizing in a high-rise corporate lab.

Introduction to Hugging Face: The Democratization of State-of-the-Art AI

Hugging Face's Transformers library is akin to a Swiss Army knife for AI developers—it's versatile, robust, and indispensable. This library provides an extensive collection of pretrained models that are the bread and butter of modern NLP tasks, from sentiment analysis and text classification to more complex tasks like question answering and summarization. The beauty of these models lies in their pretraining; they've already learned a vast amount of knowledge about language from extensive training on diverse datasets, which means you can achieve impressive results with only a fraction of the computational cost and time.

Moreover, the Datasets library acts as a catalyst for AI experimentation, providing a plethora of ready-to-use datasets that cover a wide range of applications. This offers convenience and speeds up the cycle of innovation. Researchers and developers can access high-quality data in standardized formats, allowing them to focus more on model experimentation and less on data wrangling. Whether you're looking to fine-tune a model on a niche corpus of text or test hypotheses with different data slices, Hugging Face's Datasets library is your go-to resource.

Model Hub and Community: Collaborative AI in Action

Imagine a marketplace where instead of buying and selling goods, you exchange AI models like trading cards—this is the Hugging Face model hub. Here, users can either download pretrained models contributed by others or upload their own models for the community to use. This model hub fosters a rich environment of collaboration and innovation, where both novice and experienced developers can find models that suit their specific needs, contribute to the community, and even improve existing models.

The collaborative nature of this platform allows users to exchange models and create a feedback loop where improvements, ideas, and innovations are continuously shared. This communal approach accelerates the improvement of models and the dissemination of AI advancements. For example, if you're working on a text-generation model and hit a performance snag, chances are someone in the Hugging Face community has encountered and solved a similar issue. By leveraging the community's collective knowledge, you can find solutions faster and push your projects forward more efficiently.

Fine-Tuning Models: Tailoring AI to Fit Your Needs

While pretrained models offer a fantastic starting point, the real magic happens during fine-tuning, where these models are adjusted to excel on specific tasks or datasets. Hugging Face provides tools and documentation that guide you through the fine-tuning process, making it more of an art than a science. For instance, fine-tuning a sentiment analysis model on customer reviews from a particular industry can drastically improve its accuracy and relevance as the model learns the nuances and jargon specific to that field.

The process involves adjusting the model's parameters slightly, using a smaller learning rate and your specific dataset. This method ensures that the model does not forget what it has learned during pre-training; instead, it adapts to the new data. Moreover, Hugging Face's interface simplifies this process, providing clear examples and best practices that help you fine-tune your models effectively without getting lost in the technical weeds.

Deployment Strategies: Bringing AI Models to Life

Once your models are trained and fine-tuned, the next step is deployment, and here Hugging Face shines with its flexibility. Whether you prefer deploying your models on-premise for control and security or leveraging cloud-based solutions for scalability and ease of maintenance, Hugging Face supports a range of deployment options. This flexibility allows you to choose a strategy that best fits your operational needs and technical capabilities.

For those leaning toward cloud-based solutions, Hugging Face seamlessly integrates with major cloud platforms, providing tools and APIs that help you deploy your models efficiently. This integration not only simplifies the deployment process but also ensures that your models are scalable and capable of handling varying loads without a hitch. On the other hand, if you opt for on-premise deployment, Hugging Face provides robust support and documentation that guide you through setting up your infrastructure, ensuring that your models run smoothly in a secure environment.

As you navigate the rich features and collaborative environment of Hugging Face, you'll find that it's more than just a platform—it's a catalyst for AI innovation. Whether you're fine-tuning a pretrained model, collaborating with fellow AI enthusiasts, or deploying sophisticated AI solutions, Hugging Face provides the tools, community support, and flexibility needed to bring your AI projects to fruition. Dive in, explore, and let Hugging Face be your companion in the exciting journey of AI development and deployment.

Explore Hugging Face:

4.6 AI Development With Microsoft Azure AI Tools

Overview of Azure AI Services: A Toolbox for the Modern AI Architect

Step into the realm of Microsoft Azure, where AI tools are not just abundant but meticulously crafted to cater to a wide range of needs, from those of the budding data scientist to the seasoned AI architect. Azure's suite, encompassing Azure Machine Learning, Azure Cognitive Services, and Azure Bot Services, forms a robust foundation for anyone looking to innovate with AI.

Azure Machine Learning is a powerhouse, providing a streamlined platform for building, training, and deploying machine learning models. Think of it as your AI laboratory, where you can experiment, concoct models, and swiftly move them from the drawing board to the real world without breaking a sweat. Its user-friendly interface allows you to manage the entire lifecycle of your models, from data wrangling to deployment, making it an invaluable tool for both novices and experts.

Then there's Azure Cognitive Services, which brings AI within reach without the need to be an expert in machine learning. This collection of prebuilt APIs allows for the integration of intelligent features into your applications with just a few lines of code. Whether it's adding image recognition capabilities with Computer Vision, understanding sentiment with Text Analytics, or converting speech to text with Speech Service, Cognitive Services has you covered. It's like having a Swiss Army knife for AI; whatever your needs, there's a tool ready and waiting.

Azure Bot Services rounds out the trio, enabling you to build intelligent, conversational bots that can engage with your users on a personal level. These bots can be integrated into various communication platforms such as websites, apps, email, and Microsoft Teams, making them versatile tools in enhancing user interaction and automating routine tasks.

Building and Deploying Models: From Concept to Reality

Let's dive deeper into Azure Machine Learning to understand how it transforms abstract AI concepts into tangible solutions. The process starts with the Azure Machine Learning Studio, a centralized workspace where you can construct your models using a drag-and-drop interface or by writing custom code. This flexibility allows you to work in a manner that suits your style and expertise.

Consider you're tasked with creating a predictive model for predicting stock prices. Here's how you would approach it:

1. **Data Ingestion:** Load your historical stock data into Azure Machine Learning from various sources like Azure SQL Database, Azure Blob Storage, or even external sources.

2. **Data Preparation:** Use the built-in preprocessing tools to clean and prepare your data. This might involve

normalizing the data, handling missing values, or creating new computed features.

3. **Model Training:** Select a machine learning algorithm suitable for regression tasks and configure it with your data. Azure Machine Learning supports a wide range of algorithms out-of-the-box, making this step a breeze.

4. **Evaluation and Tuning:** Once the model is trained, evaluate its performance using Azure's visualization tools. Adjust parameters or try different algorithms to improve accuracy.

5. **Deployment:** Deploy your model as a web service with just a few clicks. Azure handles the infrastructure, allowing your model to be accessed via HTTP requests from anywhere in the world.

This end-to-end workflow simplifies and accelerates the model-building process, enabling you to go from idea to deployment in record time.

Integrating Cognitive Services: Enhancing Applications With AI

Azure Cognitive Services is your go-to when you need to add AI capabilities to your applications without deep AI expertise. Integrating this service is straightforward, thanks to the comprehensive APIs and SDKs provided. For instance, if you're developing a news aggregation app and you want to incorporate sentiment analysis, you can easily plug in the Text Analytics API. Simply send your news content through the API, and receive detailed sentiment scores and emotional analysis in response.

The beauty of Cognitive Services lies in its simplicity and power; complex AI processes are distilled into simple API calls, making it possible to enhance your applications with sophisticated AI features without needing to understand the underlying models.

Leveraging Azure for Large-Scale AI: Power and Scalability at Your Fingertips

When it comes to scaling AI solutions, Azure is in its element. Its infrastructure is designed to handle large-scale deployments seamlessly, whether you're processing gigabytes of data or serving millions of API requests. Azure's global network of managed data centers ensures high availability and low latency, making your AI applications robust and responsive.

Moreover, Azure provides comprehensive security features to protect your data and models. From encrypted data storage and transfer to identity management and access controls, Azure keeps your AI assets secure at all scales. This commitment to security is crucial when deploying AI solutions that comply with stringent regulatory standards.

As you explore the capabilities of Azure AI, remember that you're leveraging a platform that supports your AI journey at every step— from building and deploying models to integrating intelligent features and scaling solutions. Whether you're a developer, a business leader, or a data scientist, Azure AI offers the power, flexibility, and support you need to transform your innovative ideas into reality, ensuring that your ventures in AI are as successful as they are groundbreaking.

As we wrap up this exploration of Azure AI tools, it's clear that the potential for innovation is limitless. With the right tools at your disposal, you can push the boundaries of what's possible with AI, creating solutions that are not only transformative but also scalable and secure. The journey through Azure AI is just one part of the larger adventure in artificial intelligence. Up next, we'll delve into other exciting aspects of AI development, ensuring that you have a well-rounded understanding of the landscape as you continue to explore and innovate. Stay tuned; the best is yet to come.

Explore Microsoft Azure:

Make a Difference with Your Review

Unlock the Power of Generosity

"Money can't buy happiness, but giving it away can." - Freddie Mercury

People who give without expecting anything in return live longer, happier lives and often find success along the way. Are you willing to assist someone unfamiliar if it meant receiving no recognition? Who is the person, you ask? They are like you. Or, at least, like you used to be. Curious, exploring new technologies, wanting to make a difference, and needing help but not sure where to look.

Our mission is to make **generative AI** knowledge accessible to everyone. All our efforts are grounded in this endeavor, intending to reach a broad audience, and this is where you play a vital part. Most people do, in fact, judge a book by its cover (and its reviews). On behalf of those aged 18 to 45 you've not met:

Your review for this book would be greatly appreciated. This small act could significantly affect others, potentially aiding local businesses, supporting entrepreneurs, or helping individuals achieve their dreams.

Your willingness to leave feedback makes a world of difference and can be accomplished easily by using this **QR code:**

Join us if making a difference anonymously resonates with you. Thank you for your consideration. Let's continue with what we were doing.

Sincerely, **Jordan Blake**

P.S. - Remember, adding value to others' lives enhances your own value to them. If you believe this book might help someone, please pass it along.

OVERCOMING CHALLENGES IN GENERATIVE AI

DATA BIAS AND FAIRNESS

DEBUGGING AND TROUBLESHOOTING

HANDLING LARGE DATASETS

EFFICIENT MODEL TRAINING

OVERCOMING OVERFITTING TECHNIQUES

MODEL SECURITY AND PRIVACY

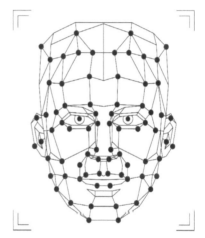

Overcoming Challenges in Generative AI

Welcome to the wild west of generative AI, where the possibilities are as vast as the challenges are daunting. Think of this chapter as your trusty guide through the AI frontier, armed with the wit of a seasoned sheriff and the tools of a savvy prospector. Here, we'll tackle one of the most notorious outlaws in the AI landscape: bias. Bias in AI is a critical flaw that can skew outcomes and perpetuate inequalities. But fear not! With the right approaches and a bit of AI know-how, you can tame this beast and ensure your AI models are fair and impartial.

5.1 Tackling Data Bias and Ensuring Fairness in AI Models

Identifying the Culprits: Sources of Bias in AI

Bias in AI can sneak in through numerous backdoors: selection bias, sampling bias, and historical bias, just to name a few notorious culprits. Selection bias occurs when the data you use to train your AI model isn't representative of the real-world scenario it's meant to address. Imagine training a facial recognition system solely on images from a vintage 1950s magazine; the results would be as outdated as the hairstyles in those photos.

Sampling bias skews your model further by influencing which data points are chosen for training. If you're developing a speech recognition system and only include voices from daytime TV shows, don't be surprised when it struggles to understand anything said in a whisper or a shout. Historical bias, the sneakiest of them all, comes from pre-existing prejudices in the data. It's like teaching your model that all swans are white because it has never seen a black swan.

Balancing the Scales: Implementing Fairness Metrics

Correcting these biases requires a robust set of fairness metrics. Think of these metrics as the scales of justice for your AI models. Equality of opportunity ensures that all individuals have a similar chance of receiving positive model predictions, regardless of their background. Demographic parity takes a broader stroke, requiring that decisions made by your model are independent of sensitive attributes like race or gender. Predictive equality, on the other hand, demands that all groups have the same false positive rates, ensuring one group isn't unfairly targeted over another.

Applying these metrics isn't just about checking boxes; it's about incorporating fairness into every aspect of your AI systems. For instance, in a hiring tool, applying equality of opportunity means that candidates are evaluated based on their qualifications, not their demographics, ensuring a level playing field for all applicants.

The Art of De-Biasing: Techniques to Cleanse Your AI

Mitigating bias in AI is akin to detoxing a poisoned well; it requires both precision and proactive measures. Techniques like resampling and reweighting adjust the balance of your training data, giving underrepresented groups a louder voice in the learning process. Algorithmic modifications, such as adversarial debiasing, introduce an element of competition, where one part of your model continuously attempts to detect bias in another, sharpening the overall accuracy and fairness.

Consider the case of a loan approval AI system trained on historical data that unintentionally favored certain demographics. By implementing resampling, the training data can be adjusted to give equal representation to all groups, thus helping to eliminate historical biases and ensuring the model assesses applicants on their merits rather than their background.

A Transparent Operation: Promoting Openness and Accountability

The final piece of the puzzle in combating bias is fostering transparency and accountability in AI development. Once you open the black box of AI algorithms, you need to build trust with those who are affected by AI decisions. Transparency involves clear documentation of how models are developed, what data is used, and how decisions are made. Accountability goes a step further, involving regular audits of AI systems and the willingness to make adjustments based on those findings.

Imagine deploying an AI system for public service allocation; transparency allows citizens to understand how decisions are made, and accountability ensures that the system continues to serve the public equitably, adjusting as community needs evolve. This open approach not only enhances the credibility of your AI systems but also aligns them more closely with societal values and ethical standards.

As we maneuver through the tangled web of bias and fairness in AI, remember that these challenges aren't insurmountable. With careful analysis, thoughtful metric implementation, and a commitment to transparency, your AI models can not only perform efficiently but also ethically. So, saddle up and let's continue this ride through the exciting yet challenging world of generative AI, ensuring our creations are as just as they are innovative.

5.2 Strategies for Efficient Model Training and Resource Management

Imagine you're a maestro orchestrating a symphony, but instead of working with ensemble members and musical notes, you're manipulating data and algorithms. Each section of your orchestra, from the violins (your algorithms) to the cellos (your computing resources), needs to be perfectly tuned and timed to create a masterpiece. But what if your violins are screechy or your cellos are off-key? That's where efficient model training and resource management come into play, making sure your AI symphony hits all the right notes without breaking the bank.

Optimizing Computational Resources: The Art of Fine-Tuning Your Orchestra

First things first, let's talk about optimizing GPU usage and memory management during model training, which can be likened to ensuring your orchestra plays harmoniously without any instrument overpowering the others. Effective batch sizing is crucial here; it's like choosing the right number of musicians for each section of the orchestra. Too few, and the sound is weak; too many, and it's overpowering. Finding the perfect batch size ensures your GPU resources are fully utilized, speeding up training without causing memory overflow.

Then there's mixed precision training, a technique that involves using different numerical precisions in the computational process. Think of it as adjusting the tension on your string instruments to get the perfect pitch—it allows for faster computations and reduces memory usage without sacrificing the quality of the output. By dynamically adjusting the precision during model training, you can significantly speed up your AI's learning rate.

Distributed computing techniques take things up a notch by splitting the computational load across multiple GPUs or even across different machines. This is akin to dividing complex pieces into sections played by different parts of the orchestra, each perfectly synchronized under your baton. Techniques like model parallelism and data parallelism allow for training larger models than what could fit in the memory of a single GPU, or they speed up training by processing data in parallel.

Managing Resource Allocation: Keeping Your Orchestra in Financial Harmony

Resource management in cloud environments can feel like trying to balance your orchestra's budget while planning a world tour. You need to ensure every dollar spent maximizes output without wasting resources. Auto-scaling services are your financial advisors here, smartly adjusting the resources allocated based on the workload. During intense training phases, these services scale up the computational power to meet demand and scale down during lulls to optimize costs.

Cost-effective resource allocation strategies also involve choosing the right type of resources for specific tasks. For instance, certain cloud services offer instances that are optimized for machine learning tasks, which might be more cost-effective than general-purpose instances. It's like hiring specialist musicians for a solo performance instead of the whole orchestra, significantly cutting costs while ensuring a stellar performance.

Implementing Efficient Training Techniques: Mastering the Composition

Advanced training techniques such as transfer learning, incremental learning, and model pruning are your composition tools, each adding depth and efficiency to your AI model's performance. Transfer learning is like using a well-known melody as the foundation for your composition, adapting it to create something new and exciting. By using a model trained on one task as the starting point for another, you reduce training time and improve model performance, especially when data is scarce.

Incremental learning, on the other hand, allows your model to learn continuously, adapting to new data without forgetting previous knowledge, just like a musician is expected to learn new pieces while retaining mastery over the classics. This is particularly useful in dynamic environments where the data evolves over time.

Model pruning is the process of trimming down the unnecessary parts of your AI model without affecting its accuracy. Think of it as cutting out the redundant or repetitive parts of your musical score, making the performance more efficient without losing the essence of the piece. This not only speeds up the training process but also reduces the computational load during inference, making the model faster and lighter.

Regularly Monitoring and Evaluating Resource Usage: Keeping Your Ensemble Sharp

The importance of continuous monitoring and evaluation of resource usage during model training cannot be overstated—it's like regularly tuning your instruments and checking the acoustics to ensure an impeccable performance. Tools and practices for monitoring resource usage help identify bottlenecks or inefficiencies in your training processes, allowing you to make informed decisions about adjustments. Whether it's reallocating resources to different tasks, adjusting batch sizes, or updating your training algorithms, regular monitoring ensures that your AI models train efficiently and cost-effectively.

In a symphony, each note must be played with precision and each resource expertly managed; this ensures that the orchestra performs at its peak. Apply this same concept when training your models: By optimizing computational resources, managing allocations judiciously, implementing advanced training techniques, and keeping a vigilant eye on operations, you orchestrate a masterpiece of efficiency and innovation. As you continue to explore AI development, remember that the harmony between speed, accuracy, and cost-efficiency is within reach, guided by these strategic insights and practices.

5.3 Overcoming Overfitting: Techniques for Model Generalization

Imagine you're prepping for the ultimate quiz show. You've only studied the questions from last year's game. Sure, you'd nail those again, but what about when the host throws a curveball question from this year? This, in a nutshell, is overfitting in the world of AI. It happens when your model performs like a champ on the training data (last year's questions) but flunks when faced with new, unseen data (this year's surprise questions). This not only cramps the style of your

AI but can lead to decisions that are about as off-key as a cat walking across a piano.

The impact? Well, overfitting makes your model a one-hit wonder. It can ace the scenarios it's seen before but struggles to generalize new data. This is a big no-no, especially in applications where flexibility and adaptability are key—like when predicting market trends or diagnosing new health conditions. Without the ability to generalize, AI models risk becoming obsolete quicker than last season's fashion trends.

Regularization Techniques: Your AI's Training Wheels

Think of regularization techniques as training wheels for your AI model—they help it stay balanced and not veer off into the overfitting ditch. L1 and L2 regularization are the cool kids on the block here. They work by adding a penalty to the loss function (think of it as a strict teacher who doesn't let you get too comfortable with just the training data). L1 regularization is like a diet plan for your model—it helps it lose unnecessary weight by pushing less important features towards zero, making the model simpler and less likely to memorize the training data. L2 regularization, on the other hand, smooths out the model parameters to avoid extreme values that could cause overfitting, ensuring your model doesn't get too swayed by the noise in the training data.

Dropout is another nifty technique. It randomly shuts down some neurons in the learning process, forcing your model to find new paths and strengthening its ability to generalize rather than obsess over specific data points. Imagine it as a pop quiz in every class—you'd need to understand the subject broadly rather than just memorizing specific lecture slides.

Early stopping is like knowing when to leave the party. It monitors the model's performance on a validation set and stops training before it begins to memorize the training data too deeply. This way, your AI learns enough to perform well but not so much that it can't adapt to new data.

The Role of Cross-Validation: No Cheating on the Test

Cross-validation is the ultimate test prep for your model. It's like taking several mock exams before the final to ensure you've got a well-rounded understanding. In k-fold cross-validation, you split your data into k number of subsets and train your model k times, each time with a different subset held out as a test set and the remaining as the training set. This method not only helps in tuning model parameters effectively but also gives a more reliable estimate of how your model will perform in the real world. It's a rigorous workout regime ensuring your model can handle whatever data it encounters, not just the data it was trained on.

Ensemble Methods: The Power of Collaboration

Lastly, let's talk about ensemble methods—because sometimes, it takes a village to raise a robust AI model. Techniques like bagging, boosting, and stacking are about teaming up multiple models for a combined prediction that's typically more accurate and robust than any single model's output. Bagging reduces variance and helps avoid overfitting by creating multiple versions of a training dataset with random sampling, training a separate model on each, and then averaging the results. Boosting, however, focuses on turning weak learners into strong ones by sequentially applying models to correct the mistakes of previous ones, similar to a tutor who helps you focus on your weak subjects. Stacking layers models like a delicious lasagna—each layer outputs predictions that feed into a final predictor, creating a combined effect that's tough to beat.

These ensemble techniques ensure that your AI model can tackle a variety of problems, much like a well-rounded student ready for any question on the exam. By leveraging the strengths of multiple learning algorithms, you enhance your model's stability and accuracy, ensuring it's not just memorizing but genuinely understanding and generalizing from the training data.

As you deploy these strategies, remember: The goal is to create AI models that aren't just good on paper but can perform reliably in the wild by adapting, learning, and thriving on new, unseen data. So, equip your AI with these techniques, and watch it navigate the complexities of real-world data with the confidence of a quiz show champion.

Test your knowledge of ensemble methods at Pro Profs:

5.4 Handling Large Datasets in AI Projects

Imagine being an urban planner tasked with designing a city that not only accommodates millions of residents but also manages their needs efficiently. In the realm of AI, handling large datasets is akin to urban planning. You must manage vast amounts of data, ensuring they're stored, processed, and utilized effectively to keep the city—your AI project—running smoothly. Let's dive into the strategies that help you manage these sprawling data metropolises.

Data Management: The Foundation of Efficient AI Architecture

Handling large datasets starts with robust data management strategies, including data partitioning, efficient storage formats, and the strategic use of data lakes and warehouses. Data partitioning is like zoning in urban planning. By segmenting your data into manageable chunks, you ensure that your AI models can process them more efficiently, much like dividing a city into residential, commercial, and industrial zones helps manage traffic and resource allocation.

Efficient data storage formats are the building codes for your data architecture. Formats like Parquet and ORC offer high compression and fast retrieval, crucial for managing large datasets without inflating storage costs or access times. Think of them as high-density, energy-efficient building designs that maximize space and resources in a bustling city.

Data lakes and warehouses serve as the central hubs of your data ecosystem. Data lakes allow for the storage of vast amounts of raw data in their native format—like a giant reservoir of every type of data you might need for your AI projects. When specific data sets are required, they can be processed and transformed for specific tasks, much like water from a reservoir being treated for different uses. Data warehouses, on the other hand, are more structured and are used for storing processed data that is ready for analysis and querying, akin to bottled water ready for consumption.

Streaming and Batching: The Highways and Byways of Data Flow

As your AI project grows, so does the influx of data, and managing this flow efficiently is crucial. Data streaming and batching are like the highways and byways of your data city, ensuring smooth and efficient traffic flow. Data streaming allows for real-time processing of data inputs, crucial for applications like live fraud detection or real-time traffic management in smart cities. Tools like Apache Kafka and Amazon Kinesis are the traffic controllers here, handling massive streams of data with ease, ensuring that your AI models receive a steady and manageable flow of information.

Batch processing, on the other hand, is like scheduled train services that handle large volumes of data at regular intervals. This method is ideal for non-time-sensitive tasks where data can be collected, stored, and processed in large batches. Tools like Apache Hadoop and Spark excel in this area, allowing for the efficient processing of large batches through their robust distributed computing capabilities. They break down data tasks into smaller, manageable parts, distribute them across a network, and process them in parallel, significantly speeding up data handling tasks.

Data Augmentation: The Urban Sprawl of AI Training

In AI, more data often translates to better models, but gathering vast amounts of training data isn't always feasible. Data augmentation strategies come to the rescue here, artificially expanding your dataset size without the need for additional real-world data. It's akin to urban sprawl in city planning, where you expand the city's area to accommodate more residents. In image processing tasks, for instance, simple techniques like rotating, flipping, or adding noise to images can create diverse training examples, helping improve the robustness of your AI models without additional data collection costs.

This technique not only enhances the diversity of your training data but also simulates a wider range of scenarios that your AI model might need to handle in the real world, making it more robust and versatile. It's like training city dwellers to thrive in both downtown hustle and suburban calm.

Scalable Data Processing Frameworks: The Infrastructure for Growth

Lastly, the backbone of any large-scale AI project is its data processing framework. Scalable frameworks like Apache Spark and Hadoop are the pillars of this infrastructure. These frameworks are designed to scale up from single servers to thousands of machines, each offering local computation and storage. This distributed nature allows them to process large datasets far more quickly than could be handled on a single machine, much like a well-designed highway system moves traffic faster and more efficiently than a single road.

These frameworks handle big data tasks, ranging from data sorting and filtering to more complex analytical queries and machine learning model training. Their ability to scale makes them indispensable for projects where data volume and velocity are high, ensuring that as your data grows, your capacity to process and analyze it grows too.

Navigating the challenges of large datasets in AI projects requires a combination of smart data management, efficient processing strategies, and robust infrastructure. By implementing these strategies, you ensure that your AI projects are not just scalable and efficient but also poised for future growth and success. As you continue to build and expand your AI capabilities, remember that the foundation you lay down now will determine the skyline of your AI city of tomorrow.

5.5 Ensuring Model Security and Privacy in Deployment

In the digital age, ensuring the security and privacy of AI models isn't just a good practice—it's imperative. Think of your AI model like a digital Fort Knox; just as you wouldn't store gold without robust security measures, you shouldn't deploy AI models without ensuring they're fortified against potential threats. Whether it's adversarial attacks that try to fool your model with deceptive data or privacy breaches that could leak sensitive information, the stakes are sky-high. But fear not: By implementing rigorous security strategies and privacy-preserving techniques, you can shield your AI applications from unwanted visitors.

Fortifying Against Invasions: Addressing Security Vulnerabilities in AI

Adversarial attacks on AI models are akin to a game of cat and mouse, where attackers continuously devise new strategies to deceive models, and defenders must adapt swiftly to mitigate these threats. One effective defense mechanism is adversarial training, which involves training your model on a mixture of regular and adversarial examples. This method is similar to a vaccine that exposes the body to a weakened virus to build immunity; it helps the model learn to recognize and resist potential attacks, making it robust against adversarial inputs.

Robustness testing takes this a step further by continuously testing and retesting the AI model against potential vulnerabilities. Think of it as a stress test for your AI's immune system, ensuring it can withstand adversarial attacks under different conditions. This ongoing process helps identify weaknesses in the model's armor, allowing you to reinforce it before attackers can exploit these vulnerabilities.

Safeguarding Secrets: Implementing Privacy-Preserving Techniques

As AI continues to permeate various sectors, the importance of maintaining privacy in AI applications has skyrocketed. Techniques like differential privacy, federated learning, and homomorphic encryption are the superheroes of the AI privacy world. Differential privacy, for instance, adds noise to the data used in training the AI model, masking individual contributions without significantly affecting the overall outcome. This is akin to blending individual voices in a choir—the harmony remains, but individual voices aren't distinguishable.

Federated learning takes a different approach by decentralizing the data processing. Instead of bringing all data to one central point, it trains algorithms locally on users' devices and only shares the insights gained, not the data itself. This method not only helps preserve privacy but also reduces the bandwidth needed for data transfer, akin to having local rehearsals in various neighborhoods before bringing the choir together for the final performance.

Homomorphic encryption is perhaps the most magical of all, allowing data to be processed in an encrypted form, providing results without ever exposing the underlying data. It's like being able to unlock a treasure chest and use the gold inside while keeping it safely locked away.

Locking Down the Fort: Best Practices for Secure Model Deployment

Deploying AI models securely involves more than just robust training; it requires a secure environment every step of the way. Utilizing secure containers for deploying AI models ensures that each model operates in a controlled environment, isolated from others, much like safe deposit boxes in a bank. These containers protect the model and its data from unauthorized access and interference, maintaining the integrity and confidentiality of the AI application.

API security is another critical aspect, especially when AI functionalities are accessed through APIs. Implementing measures such as authentication, rate limiting, and encryption ensures that only authorized users can access the API, and data remains secure during transmission. Continuous security monitoring keeps a vigilant eye on the system, ready to alert you to any suspicious activity, much like security cameras and alarms in a bank.

Upholding the Law: Navigating the Maze of Regulations

Compliance with privacy laws and ethical standards is not just about avoiding legal repercussions; it's about building trust and credibility in your AI systems. Regulations like the General Data Protection Regulation (GDPR) in the EU and the California Consumer Privacy Act (CCPA) in the US set strict guidelines on data privacy and user rights. Adhering to these regulations requires a thorough understanding of the legal landscape and a proactive approach to data privacy.

Implementing privacy by design, conducting regular privacy impact assessments, and maintaining transparent data usage policies are essential steps in ensuring compliance. These measures not only help avoid costly legal battles but also reassure users that their data is in safe hands, fostering a positive relationship between your AI application and its users.

Securing AI models and preserving privacy are critical components of deploying robust and trustworthy AI systems. By addressing security vulnerabilities, implementing privacy-preserving techniques, ensuring secure deployment, and complying with legal standards, you can protect your AI models from threats and misuse, ensuring they serve their intended purpose without compromising security or privacy. As AI continues to evolve, staying ahead of these challenges is crucial for anyone looking to leverage AI technology responsibly and effectively.

5.6 Debugging and Troubleshooting Generative AI Models

Unraveling the Tangles: Common Issues in AI Models

Navigating the labyrinth of generative AI development is akin to untangling a set of Christmas lights—you know the outcome will be brilliant, but the process can be fraught with challenges. Key among these are data leakage, model drift, and convergence problems, each capable of dimming the sparkle of your AI projects. Data leakage occurs when information from outside the training dataset is used to create the model, inadvertently giving the model a cheat sheet for its future exams. This can result in overly optimistic performance measures during training, only to disappoint in real-world applications.

Model drift, on the other hand, is the sneaky character that gradually changes the underlying relationships in the data over time, making the once-brilliant model slowly obsolete. Imagine teaching your model all about the world of flip phones only for smartphones to take over the market.

Lastly, convergence problems arise when your model training goes on a never-ending spiral and fails to reach a satisfactory result, much like a car stuck in a mud pit spinning its wheels.

Tools of the Trade: Debugging Tools and Techniques

To combat these issues, a robust arsenal of debugging tools and techniques is your best ally. Model visualization tools allow you to peek inside the AI's decision-making process, turning abstract numbers into understandable visuals. These tools can highlight areas where the model is focusing incorrectly, helping you pinpoint where things are going awry. Logging, on the other hand, is like keeping a detailed diary of the model's life. By recording data about the model's performance and behavior over time, you can track down when and where the model started to deviate from the expected path.

Diagnostic algorithms act as the AI's physicians, diagnosing problems and prescribing solutions. These algorithms can analyze the model's structure and operations, identifying inefficiencies and errors that aren't immediately obvious. Together, these tools not only help in pinpointing the issues but also play a crucial role in understanding why these issues occur, paving the way for more effective solutions.

A Method to the Madness: Systematic Troubleshooting Approaches

When it comes to troubleshooting AI models, systematic approaches are like following a treasure map with precision. Hypothesis-driven debugging is one such approach. First, you start with a theory— perhaps you suspect that data leakage is due to how the training dataset is split. You then test this hypothesis by altering the dataset handling and observing if the model's performance improves in a controlled test. Similarly, ablation studies involve systematically removing parts of the model or data inputs to see their impact on the model's performance. This method helps isolate the elements that are critical for the model's success or are potential sources of trouble.

These structured approaches ensure that you're not just randomly tweaking your model but are making informed adjustments based on solid evidence, significantly increasing the efficiency of your troubleshooting efforts.

Cultivating Excellence: Promoting a Culture of Testing and Validation

In the high-octane world of generative AI, a culture of rigorous testing and validation is the safety net that prevents your projects from crashing and burning. This culture emphasizes the importance of thorough testing at every stage of the AI development lifecycle. Unit testing ensures that individual components of your AI system function correctly, while integration testing checks that these components work well together. A/B testing, or split testing, is particularly useful in fine-tuning AI models, as it allows you to compare different versions of your model to determine which performs best under real-world conditions.

Incorporating these testing methodologies not only bolsters the reliability and performance of your AI models but also instills a discipline of continuous improvement and quality assurance within your team. By regularly validating your models and integrating feedback into the development process, you ensure that your AI solutions are not only effective but also resilient and adaptable to changing conditions.

As we wrap up this exploration of debugging and troubleshooting in generative AI, remember that the path to a robust and reliable AI model is paved with challenges. However, with the right tools, techniques, and a culture of rigorous testing, these challenges can be systematically identified, diagnosed, and remedied. By embracing these practices, you ensure that your AI projects are not just technically sound but also strategically poised for success in the ever-evolving landscape of artificial intelligence. Now, let's gear up and dive into the next chapter, where we'll explore the exciting world of AI applications in dynamic environments, pushing the boundaries of what AI can achieve in real-time scenarios.

ETHICAL CONSIDERATIONS AND RESPONSIBLE AI

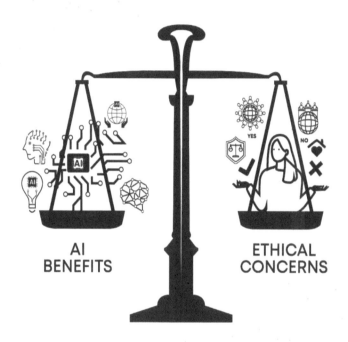

AI
BENEFITS

ETHICAL
CONCERNS

Chapter 6:

Ethical Considerations and Responsible AI

Navigating the ethical landscape of generative AI is like walking a tightrope while juggling—both thrilling and fraught with potential pitfalls. As we delve into this complex topic, consider yourself armed with a moral compass and a keen sense of balance. Here, we'll explore the intricacies and responsibilities that come with wielding the powerful tool that is AI, ensuring that as we stride forward, we do so with both wisdom and caution.

6.1 Navigating the Ethical Landscape of Generative AI

Understanding Ethical Dilemmas: The Conundrums of Creativity

Generative AI, like any powerful tool, comes with its share of ethical dilemmas that can puzzle the unprepared. Take deepfakes, for instance—these hyper-realistic fabrications made possible by AI can blur the lines between truth and deception, challenging our very perception of reality. What happens when a deepfake video of a political leader declaring war goes viral? The implications are as serious as they are terrifying, raising alarms about privacy violations and the spread of misinformation.

But the ethical rabbit hole goes deeper. Consider AI-generated art. Who owns the rights to a piece of art created by AI? Is it the creator of the AI, the user who provided the initial input, or the AI itself? And let's not forget about the potential for AI to perpetuate biases, a concern that looms large as these technologies become gatekeepers in areas as critical as hiring and law enforcement. Each of these scenarios underscores the pressing need for ethical vigilance as we integrate these advanced technologies into the sinews of society.

Establishing Ethical Frameworks: Creating the Rule Book

Just as every game needs its rules to prevent chaos, the field of generative AI requires robust ethical frameworks to guide its use. Organizations like the IEEE and the Future of Life Institute have been at the forefront, drafting guidelines that address everything from ensuring transparency in AI systems to safeguarding against malicious use. These frameworks are not just academic exercises; they are blueprints that help developers, users, and policymakers navigate the ethical minefield of AI, ensuring that these technologies are used for the greater good.

Adopting these guidelines involves a commitment to ethical AI development, which includes testing rigorously for biases, designing for privacy, and ensuring that AI systems are transparent and understandable to users. By adhering to these frameworks, developers not only build trust with users but also fortify their creations against ethical missteps that could lead to public backlash or legal troubles.

Engaging With Stakeholders: The Power of Diverse Perspectives

The ethical use of AI is not a puzzle to be solved in isolation. It requires the engagement of a broad spectrum of stakeholders, from ethicists and sociologists to end-users and policymakers. Each group brings a unique perspective that can illuminate potential risks and ethical considerations that might not be apparent to AI developers alone.

For instance, public consultations can uncover societal concerns about AI, such as fears about job displacement or privacy invasions, which can then be addressed directly in the AI's design. Collaborations with ethicists can help parse complex moral issues, ensuring that AI systems align with broader human values. By fostering an inclusive dialogue around the development and deployment of AI technologies, we ensure that these systems are not only technologically sound but also socially responsible.

Promoting Ethical Literacy: Educating the AI Workforce

As generative AI continues to evolve, so too must our understanding of its ethical implications. This is where ethical literacy comes into play—it's about equipping AI professionals with the technical skills to build AI and the ethical acumen to foresee and forestall potential misuses.

Educational programs that integrate ethics into the AI curriculum are crucial in cultivating a generation of AI developers who are as adept at navigating ethical dilemmas as they are at coding. Workshops, seminars, and courses on AI ethics should be a staple in the education of every AI professional, ensuring that they understand the societal impacts of the technologies they create. This isn't just about avoiding pitfalls; it's about empowering these professionals to use AI as a force for good, crafting technologies that enhance our lives while respecting our values.

As we chart our course through the ethical landscape of generative AI, let us be guided by a commitment to thoughtful, inclusive, and responsible AI development. By understanding the ethical dilemmas at play, establishing robust frameworks, engaging with diverse stakeholders, and promoting ethical literacy, we ensure that our journey with AI advances humanity, not hinders it. Let's wield this powerful tool with both the foresight of what it can accomplish and the wisdom to use it well.

6.2 Developing AI With Transparency and Accountability

Implementing Transparency Mechanisms: The Clear Glass Approach

In the realm of generative AI, operating with transparency isn't just about showing off the inner workings—it's about building trust and understanding, much like a glass-walled kitchen in a high-end restaurant. You wouldn't eat at a place where the food is prepared in secrecy, and similarly, AI systems should not operate in a black box. Transparency in AI involves clear documentation of AI processes and decision-making pathways. This means every step, from the initial data input to the final decision output, should be outlined and accessible not just to the data scientists but also to the end-users. Imagine a scenario where an AI system denies a loan application. The applicant has every right to know how this decision was made. Detailed documentation that explains the data points considered and the weights assigned to each ensures that decisions made by AI are not perceived as arbitrary but are understandable and, if necessary, contestable.

Furthermore, visual tools and dashboards can play a crucial role in demystifying AI operations. These tools can translate complex algorithms into intuitive graphs and charts, making it easier for non-experts to grasp how decisions are being made. Just as a GPS shows you the route, traffic conditions, and your estimated time of arrival, these visualizations provide a roadmap of the AI decision-making process, enhancing transparency and fostering a deeper understanding of AI systems.

Ensuring Accountability in AI Systems: Keeping AI in Check

Keeping AI accountable is like ensuring that all players in a game adhere to the rules, and if they don't, systems are in place to address any issues. Accountability in AI can be achieved through various mechanisms such as audit trails, third-party audits, and the establishment of AI ethics boards. Audit trails are digital breadcrumbs that record every step taken by an AI system, providing a historical record that can be traced back if something goes awry. This not only helps in pinpointing the source of any problem but also serves as a deterrent against potential misuse of AI technologies.

Third-party audits, conducted by independent bodies, are akin to periodic health inspections for restaurants. Just as these inspections ensure a restaurant maintains hygiene standards, third-party audits verify that AI systems adhere to ethical standards and regulations, providing an unbiased assessment of AI practices. Meanwhile, AI ethics boards function like regulatory bodies in professional sports, setting the standards and best practices for AI development and use. Comprising experts from diverse fields, these boards evaluate AI projects to ensure they meet ethical guidelines and are aligned with societal values.

Promoting Open-Source AI Models: Community at the Core

The open-source movement in AI is the digital equivalent of a communal garden where everyone contributes to and benefits from a shared plot of land. By encouraging the use of open-source AI models, we advocate for a collaborative approach where AI advancements are not held behind corporate gates but are accessible to everyone. This democratizes AI development, allowing developers from around the world to review, improve, and innovate upon existing models. Such transparency not only accelerates the pace of AI innovation but also reduces the risks of hidden biases as the diverse global community continuously scrutinizes and refines the models.

Open-source models thrive on community contributions, which in turn fosters a more inclusive AI development environment. This inclusivity is crucial in tackling biases as it brings a multitude of perspectives into AI development, ensuring that the models are robust and fair. Moreover, the collaborative nature of open-source projects encourages a culture of learning and sharing, strengthening the overall ecosystem of AI development.

Creating Explainable AI: No More Magic Tricks

Explainable AI (XAI) is about turning the "magic" of AI into something more akin to a well-documented science experiment. XAI aims to make AI decisions comprehensible to humans, providing clear explanations of how inputs are transformed into outputs. This is crucial for building trust and maintaining compliance with regulations such as the GDPR, which includes a right to explanation. By implementing XAI, we ensure that AI systems are not just efficient but also understandable and justifiable.

Developing explainable AI involves using techniques that inherently provide more transparency. For instance, decision tree-based models inherently offer more explainability than neural networks, as the decision paths can be easily traced and understood. Additionally, techniques such as feature importance scoring can help illuminate which inputs most significantly impact the outputs, providing insights into the decision-making process of more complex models.

As we continue to integrate AI into various sectors of society, ensuring that these systems operate with transparency and accountability is paramount. By implementing robust transparency mechanisms, ensuring accountability through audits and ethics boards, promoting open-source models, and developing explainable AI, we lay down a framework that supports ethical AI development. This framework not only fosters trust among users but also ensures that AI technologies are used responsibly and beneficially, paving the way for a future where AI and humanity progress hand in hand.

Explore explainable AI with BertViz's attention visualization tool:

6.3 Bias Mitigation Techniques in AI Training

Let's roll up our sleeves and get into the nitty-gritty of bias mitigation in AI training, a task as crucial as ensuring a level playing field in a high-stakes game. Just as a slight tilt in the ground can skew the entire game, unnoticed biases in AI training can lead to skewed outcomes, favoring some while unfairly disadvantaging others. The process starts with the identification and assessment of these biases, followed by inclusive data collection practices, the integration of debiasing algorithms, and the relentless pursuit of continuous monitoring.

Identifying and Assessing Biases: Playing Detective With Your Data

Think of yourself as a detective when it comes to identifying and assessing biases in your AI datasets. Advanced detection tools and statistical techniques can help you sniff out biases that might be lurking in the shadows of your data. These tools scan through your dataset, looking for patterns or anomalies that could indicate bias, such as disproportionate representation of certain groups or predictive inaccuracies that skew towards specific demographics.

Statistical analysis plays a crucial role here. Techniques like regression analysis can help you understand how different variables in your data, such as age, gender, or race, affect your model's predictions. It's about asking questions like: Does the model predict loan approval more favorably for one demographic group over another, even when other variables are held constant? By rigorously testing and analyzing your data, you can unearth hidden biases and set the stage for more equitable AI models.

Implementing Inclusive Data Collection: Casting a Wider Net

If bias detection is about finding flaws, inclusive data collection is about fixing the foundation. It ensures that the data you feed into your AI models reflects the rich tapestry of human demographics and experiences. This means not only including diverse data points but also ensuring that these points accurately represent the broader population.

Think about how a wide-angle lens captures more of a scene than a narrow one. In a similar vein, inclusive data practices expand the scope of your data collection to include underrepresented groups, ensuring their perspectives and realities are not overlooked. This might involve partnering with organizations that work closely with these groups or using stratified sampling techniques to ensure all segments of the population are included in your training data. The goal is to create a dataset that mirrors the diversity of the real world, thus enabling the AI to make decisions that are fair and relevant to all.

Adopting Debiasing Algorithms: The AI Equalizers

Once you've identified potential biases and gathered a more inclusive dataset, the next step is to implement debiasing algorithms. These algorithms are the equalizers, adjusting the scales to balance out any remaining biases in your data or model. One popular technique is the reweighting of examples, where the algorithm assigns different weights to training examples based on how underrepresented they are in the data. This ensures that the model pays more attention to these examples during training, helping to counteract any existing biases.

Another approach is to modify the algorithm itself to make it less sensitive to biased patterns in the data. For instance, some algorithms can be tweaked to ignore variables that are likely to create bias, such as zip codes in a housing loan application, which might correlate with racial demographics. By carefully adjusting these algorithms, you can steer your AI away from discriminatory decision-making paths and towards more equitable outcomes.

Continuous Monitoring for Biases: Keeping AI in Check

The final, ongoing challenge in bias mitigation is the continuous monitoring of AI systems. Just as societal norms and values evolve, so too must our AI systems adapt to remain fair and unbiased over time. Continuous monitoring involves regularly reviewing and updating the AI models to ensure they do not develop or perpetuate biases as they interact with new data and changing environments.

This process can be likened to a feedback loop where AI systems are routinely tested for biases, and adjustments are made as needed. Tools like AI auditing platforms can automate this process, providing regular reports on how the AI is performing across different demographics and flagging any areas where biases may be creeping in. This proactive approach not only maintains the integrity of your AI systems but also builds trust with users by demonstrating a commitment to fairness and equity.

As we work through the intricacies of AI bias mitigation, it's clear that this is not a one-time fix but a continuous commitment to ethical AI development. By identifying and assessing biases, implementing inclusive data collection practices, adopting debiasing algorithms, and engaging in continuous monitoring, we ensure that our AI systems serve all of humanity, not just a privileged few. Now, let's move forward, keeping these principles at the forefront as we continue to explore the expansive possibilities of AI.

6.4 Privacy Enhancements in AI Applications

Mastering the Art of Data Anonymization: Keeping Your Secrets Safe

In the bustling digital marketplace of today, where data is as precious as gold, ensuring the privacy of this data can be thought of as locking your treasures in a vault. Data anonymization techniques such as data masking and k-anonymity serve as sophisticated locks that keep your data safe from prying eyes while still allowing valuable insights to be gleaned. Data masking, for example, is the digital equivalent of a masquerade ball. It disguises sensitive data by replacing it with fictional but plausible alternatives. Whether it's obscuring personal identifiers in a dataset or transforming financial records to maintain confidentiality, data masking ensures that privacy is preserved even when data is accessed by multiple stakeholders across various platforms.

Then there's k-anonymity, a technique that ensures that individual records in a dataset cannot be distinguished from at least k-1 other records regarding specific identifying attributes. Imagine you're at a party where at least k people are wearing the same costume. Identifying any individual becomes significantly more challenging, doesn't it? Similarly, k-anonymity in data sets increases privacy by making it difficult to link data back to individuals without affecting the utility of the data for analysis and decision-making. This method is particularly valuable in fields like healthcare or financial services, where personal data is sensitive but essential for developing predictive models or tailoring services to individual needs.

Leveraging Cutting-Edge Privacy Technologies: Federated Learning and Secure Multi-Party Computation

As we more deeply investigate AI, traditional data privacy methods often fall short, especially when it comes to training sophisticated AI models that require access to vast amounts of data. Enter advanced technologies like federated learning and secure multi-party computation, which are the superheroes of privacy-preserving AI technologies. Federated learning, for instance, allows AI models to be trained directly on your device, such as your smartphone or tablet. The training data never leaves the device, and only the learned insights (not the data itself) are shared to improve the model. This method not only keeps your data private but also utilizes the collective learning from thousands of devices, resulting in a model that is both robust and respectful of user privacy.

Secure multi-party computation (MPC) takes this a step further by allowing multiple parties to jointly compute a function over their inputs while keeping those inputs private. Imagine a group of competitors who want to find out who has the highest sales without revealing their actual sales figures to each other. MPC would allow them to do just that, preserving the confidentiality of their data while still enabling the necessary calculations for comparison. In the context of AI, MPC can be used to train models on combined datasets from multiple sources without any party having access to the others' data, ensuring privacy and security are maintained.

Establishing Strong Data Governance Policies: The Rulebook for Data Use

To truly safeguard privacy in AI applications, robust data governance policies that regulate access to and use of data are non-negotiable. These policies are the rulebooks that dictate who can access data, how it can be used, and under what circumstances. Implementing strong data governance involves setting clear guidelines for data handling, establishing strict access controls, and regularly auditing data use to ensure compliance with privacy laws and standards. It's like having a set of traffic rules for data flow within an organization, ensuring that every bit of data moves in an orderly, secure, and ethical manner.

These governance policies not only protect sensitive information but also build trust among users by demonstrating a commitment to data privacy and security. In an era where data breaches can erode user trust and result in significant financial and reputational damage, having a solid data governance framework is not just beneficial; it's essential.

Promoting User Control Over Data: Empowering the Digital Citizen

In the digital age, empowering users with control over their data is less of a courtesy and more of a right. Promoting user control means providing mechanisms for users to understand what data is collected and how it is used and giving them the ability to influence this process. This includes options to opt-out of data collection, tools to access and review personal data, and the ability to correct or delete this information if desired.

Such transparency and control not only comply with privacy regulations like GDPR but also empower users, giving them a say in the digital ecosystem. As AI continues to permeate various aspects of our lives, ensuring that users can assert control over their data is crucial for maintaining privacy and autonomy in the face of increasingly intelligent and pervasive technology systems.

As we continue to harness the power of AI, integrating robust privacy-enhancing techniques and policies is crucial. By adopting data anonymization methods, leveraging advanced privacy-preserving technologies, establishing strong data governance frameworks, and promoting user control over data, we ensure that AI serves as a tool for enhancement rather than a threat to privacy. Let's move forward, keeping these principles at the forefront as we continue to explore the expansive possibilities of AI.

6.5 The Role of AI in Society: Benefits and Residual Risks

Illuminating the Bright Side: AI's Societal Superpowers

Imagine a world where AI isn't just a gadget in your smart home but a powerhouse solving some of the most pressing societal challenges. From healthcare to education, transportation to environmental management, the potential of AI to improve quality of life is immense and undeniable. In healthcare, AI is like a high-tech doctor's assistant, analyzing vast amounts of data to diagnose diseases with astonishing accuracy and speed. It's not just about faster diagnostics; AI can tailor treatments to individual genetic profiles, making personalized medicine a widespread reality, not just a sci-fi fantasy.

In the education sector, AI transforms traditional learning by personalizing education to fit the unique needs of each student. Think of it as a tutor who understands exactly where a student struggles and adapts their teaching methods in real time to suit their learning pace and style. This capability is revolutionizing education, making learning more accessible and effective, particularly in underserved communities where educational resources are scarce.

Transportation is another arena where AI shines, optimizing everything from traffic management to fuel usage, reducing congestion, and minimizing emissions. Smart traffic management systems can predict and manage traffic flow more efficiently, drastically reducing the time spent on commutes and the carbon footprint of vehicles. Moreover, AI-driven predictive maintenance ensures public transport vehicles operate at peak efficiency, reducing downtime and repair costs.

Addressing the Shadows: Navigating AI's Potential Pitfalls

However, with great power comes great responsibility, and the power of AI is no exception. The advancements brought by AI are accompanied by significant risks and challenges that need careful consideration and management. One of the most pressing concerns is job displacement. As AI systems become increasingly capable, they can perform tasks traditionally done by humans, leading to concerns about widespread job losses in sectors like manufacturing, customer service, and even professional fields such as law and journalism. It's crucial to consider how we can re-skill and upskill the workforce to thrive in an AI-enhanced future, ensuring that AI acts as a job creator rather than just a job displacer.

Surveillance and privacy are other dark aspects of AI development. As AI technologies become more integrated into everyday life, the potential for invasive data collection and surveillance increases. This can lead to a "surveillance state" scenario where personal freedoms are compromised. Balancing the benefits of AI-powered monitoring systems, such as those used for public safety or health tracking, with the need to protect individual privacy rights is a delicate dance that requires thoughtful regulation and oversight.

Moreover, AI can exacerbate social inequalities if not managed carefully. For instance, if AI systems are trained on data that reflect existing biases, they can perpetuate and even amplify these biases. An AI system used for screening job applicants might prefer candidates from a certain demographic background simply because it was trained on data reflecting past hiring practices, inadvertently perpetuating historical injustices.

Championing Sustainable AI Development: Thinking Long-Term

As we harness AI's potential to transform society, it's imperative to advocate for sustainable AI development practices. This means developing AI systems that are not only effective but also sustainable in terms of their environmental, social, and economic impact. For example, AI can be used to optimize energy use in data centers, reducing the carbon footprint of the very technology that drives them. In agriculture, AI-driven precision farming can minimize waste and enhance yield, using resources like water and fertilizers more efficiently and sustainably.

Preventing technological monopolies is another critical aspect of sustainable AI development. As AI technologies become central to economic and social infrastructures, it's vital to prevent too much power from being concentrated in the hands of a few tech giants. Promoting open-source AI projects and supporting policies that encourage competition and innovation in the AI sector are essential steps to ensure that the benefits of AI are distributed widely and fairly across society.

Fostering Responsible Innovation: Aligning AI with Human Values

Lastly, responsible innovation in AI is about ensuring that the development and deployment of AI technologies align with societal values and ethical principles. This involves not only adhering to ethical guidelines but also actively engaging with diverse communities to understand their needs and concerns. AI technologies should be developed with a clear understanding of the cultural, social, and ethical contexts in which they will operate.

Encouraging a culture of responsible innovation among AI developers and companies fosters an environment where ethical considerations are at the forefront of technology design and deployment. This approach mitigates the risks associated with AI; it also enhances its acceptance and integration into society, ensuring that AI technologies are used as a force for good, enhancing human capabilities and improving lives across the globe.

As we continue to explore and expand the capabilities of AI, let us move forward with a balanced perspective, embracing its potential to transform society while vigilantly navigating the challenges it presents. By promoting sustainable development practices, advocating for responsible innovation, and aligning AI with human values, we can harness this formidable technology to create a future where both technology and humanity prosper together, advancing side by side toward a brighter, more equitable world.

6.6 Future-Proofing AI Ethics: Long-Term Considerations

Preparing for Tomorrow's Ethical Challenges

As we stand at the precipice of an AI-infused future, it's crucial to peer into the horizon and anticipate the ethical challenges that lie ahead. Imagine a scenario where AI systems not only make decisions but also interpret and modify the rules of decision-making themselves. Advanced AI autonomy, a concept that might seem plucked from science fiction, is inching closer to reality. As these technologies gain the ability to act independently, the stakes get exponentially higher in ensuring they align with ethical norms and human values.

This proactive stance involves grappling with complex questions about the delegation of decision-making to AI systems, especially in critical areas such as military applications or life-and-death medical decisions. The risk of abdicating too much control to AI systems or the emergence of "black box" decision-making processes where the rationale is not transparent pose significant ethical concerns. By anticipating these challenges, we can sculpt guidelines and regulations that ensure AI systems enhance human decision-making rather than replace it, maintaining a balance where technology supports but does not overshadow human judgment.

Advocating for Adaptive Ethical Frameworks

The only constant in technology is change, and in the landscape of AI, this change is both rapid and profound. In response, ethical frameworks governing AI must be equally dynamic, capable of evolving alongside technological advancements. Static ethical guidelines risk becoming obsolete as new AI technologies emerge and societal norms shift. Therefore, advocating for the development of adaptive ethical frameworks is akin to building an agile and responsive governance system for AI.

These frameworks should be designed to update automatically as new ethical dilemmas arise and should be flexible enough to accommodate different cultural and social contexts. For instance, what is considered an invasion of privacy in one culture may be viewed as a necessary security measure in another. Adaptive frameworks ensure that ethical guidelines remain relevant and effective, providing a scaffolding that supports the responsible development and deployment of AI technologies globally.

Fostering International Collaboration

AI technology knows no borders, and its impact is global. As such, international collaboration is paramount in creating universal standards and norms for AI ethics. This collaboration involves governments, international organizations, academia, and the private sector. The goal is to forge a consensus on ethical AI practices that transcend national interests and reflect a shared commitment to upholding human dignity and rights.

Imagine a United Nations of AI Ethics, where international leaders convene to agree on core principles like transparency, fairness, and accountability in AI. Such collaborative efforts could lead to the development of a global ethical AI treaty, similar to the Paris Agreement on climate change, which sets out clear commitments and accountability mechanisms to guide the ethical development of AI technologies worldwide.

Cultivating an Ethical AI Culture

Finally, the cornerstone of future-proofing AI ethics lies in cultivating an ethical culture within organizations and industries that develop and deploy AI technologies. This culture is nurtured through ongoing ethical training, awareness programs, and a commitment to ethical practices at every level of the organization—from the boardroom to the development lab.

Creating an ethical AI culture means embedding ethical considerations into the DNA of organizational processes, encouraging employees to think critically about the ethical implications of their work, and rewarding ethical decision-making. AI ethics training modules, ethical decision-making frameworks, and ethics officers in organizations can play pivotal roles in fostering this culture. By ingraining ethical awareness into the fabric of the AI industry, we ensure that ethical considerations are front and center in the development and deployment of AI technologies, rather than an afterthought.

As we wrap up this journey through the ethical considerations of AI, let's carry forward the insights and strategies discussed here. By preparing for future challenges, advocating for adaptive frameworks, fostering international collaboration, and cultivating an ethical culture, we lay down a robust foundation for an AI-augmented future that respects and enhances human values. Now, as we turn the page to the next chapter, let us continue to explore the vast possibilities of AI, guided by the principles of responsible and ethical innovation.

CAREER ADVANCEMENT IN AI

Chapter 7:

Career Advancement in AI

Picture this: You're at a grand AI-themed masquerade ball, and the room is buzzing with characters from every corner of the AI world. Some hide their identity behind sparkly "Data Scientist" masks, while others wear intricate "Machine Learning Engineer" veils. Welcome to the exciting world of AI careers, where the possibilities are as varied as the masks at a Venetian ball. It's here that you'll depart on a thrilling career journey that takes you on an exploration of entry-level positions to the illustrious heights of AI mastery.

7.1 Mapping Out AI Career Paths: From Beginner to Expert

Understanding Career Stages: The Stepping Stones of AI Careers

Starting as an AI intern or analyst is like being handed the keys to the kingdom, albeit the outer gardens. Here, you're expected to familiarize yourself with the landscape—learning the basics of algorithms and data patterns, and perhaps, making your first tentative tweaks to machine learning models. It's about building a solid foundation, much like learning to play scales before you can perform a Chopin nocturne at a concert.

As you ascend to roles like AI Developer or Data Scientist, you're no longer just observing—you're making the magic happen. This is where you apply your skills to create algorithms that can predict, analyze, and learn with increasing complexity. Each project is a stepping stone, each challenge a chance to sharpen your skills. You're the sorcerer's apprentice, but now with enough knowledge to not flood the workshop!

Reaching the zenith of your career path might see you become an AI Architect or a Research Scientist, roles that come with the heavy responsibility of not just following trends but setting them. Here, you're tasked with overseeing significant projects, pioneering research, or leading teams to innovate uses of AI that haven't been thought of before. In these roles, the responsibilities, challenges, and rewards are all equally exciting.

Highlighting Key Roles and Responsibilities: What It Really Takes

Navigating through the AI career maze requires more than just technical prowess; it demands creativity, analytical thinking, and an ethical compass. As an AI Intern, your role might involve data cleaning—a humble yet crucial task to ensure the data feeding into models isn't muddied by inconsistencies. Move up to a Machine Learning Engineer, and you're designing the models themselves, deciding which algorithms best predict customer behavior or optimize business processes.

For those donning the AI Architect mask, the responsibilities broaden dramatically. You're not just building models but also ensuring they integrate seamlessly with existing IT systems, align with business goals, and adhere to ethical guidelines. It's about having a bird's-eye view of the AI landscape and making strategic decisions that will influence not just your company but potentially the broader field of AI.

Exploring Career Trajectories: The Many Paths of AI

The beauty of a career in AI is its dynamic nature—there's no one prescribed path but rather a multitude of trajectories one can take. Perhaps you started in software development but found your niche in AI by applying those coding skills to machine learning projects. Or maybe your journey began in a different realm—biology, finance, or arts—and you discovered that AI could magnify your impact in these fields.

Interestingly, AI careers do not always follow a straightforward trajectory. You might find yourself moving laterally, from a specialist in natural language processing to a role focusing on ethical AI implementations, ensuring that AI technologies are used responsibly. Or you might climb vertically, where one day you're a team member, and the next, you're leading the team.

Real-Life Career Stories: Learning From Those Who've Walked the Path

Consider Elena, who started her career as a data analyst at a tech startup. Her fascination with predictive analytics led her to pursue further studies in machine learning, eventually propelling her into a role as a Senior AI Researcher. Today, she leads her own team, developing AI tools that help diagnose diseases faster and more accurately.

Then there's Jay, whose background in video game design offered him a unique perspective on AI. He leveraged his skills to move into AI-driven interactive media, where he now works on creating adaptive learning environments that respond to the learner's engagement level and learning style.

Each story is a testament to the vibrant, ever-evolving landscape of AI careers, filled with challenges to overcome and opportunities to seize.

As you plot your own course in this exciting field, remember that each step, whether a steep climb or a lateral stride, is a move towards greater mastery and understanding of AI. With the right mix of skills, curiosity, and determination, the paths you can take are as limitless as your ambition. So, adjust your mask and step confidently into the grand ballroom of AI careers. The dance of your life awaits.

7.2 The Rise of AI Specializations: Identifying Your Niche

In the world of AI, specialization is the spice that can transform a bland resume into a captivating career saga. Picture AI as a sprawling metropolis, with each district—whether Machine Learning Engineering or AI Ethics or AI in Healthcare—boasting its own unique flavor and culture. Understanding these specializations is akin to being a culinary critic; you need to taste (explore) each one to truly appreciate and decide which one suits your palate (career aspirations).

Introducing AI Specializations: A Tour of the AI Metropolis

Let's start with Machine Learning Engineering, a bustling district where algorithms are king. In this domain, professionals focus on developing systems that can learn from and make decisions based on data. Dive deeper, and you'll find sub-specialties like deep learning and reinforcement learning, each with its own set of challenges and rewards.

Next, stroll through the serene lanes of AI Ethics, where philosophers meet programmers. This specialization deals with the moral implications of AI technologies—ensuring they serve humanity's best interests. Professionals here work on developing guidelines that help prevent biases in AI models, ensuring that AI solutions are fair and equitable.

Venture into the world of AI in Healthcare, where AI meets anatomy. This sector is revolutionizing medicine by providing more accurate diagnoses, personalized treatment plans, and robotic surgical assistance. It's a field where your work directly contributes to saving lives, offering a profound sense of purpose and fulfillment.

Assessing Skills and Interests: Finding Your AI Calling

Identifying which AI specialization aligns with your skills and interests can sometimes feel like trying to solve a complex algorithm. Start by conducting a self-assessment—list your technical skills, such as coding languages or software proficiency, and soft skills, like problem-solving or ethical reasoning. Tools like online quizzes or career aptitude tests can also provide insights into which AI fields might suit you best.

Reflect on your passions and the sectors that excite you. Are you intrigued by the ethical questions raised by AI? Or perhaps the healthcare applications of AI pique your interest? Aligning your career with your interests not only leads to greater job satisfaction but can also fuel your motivation to excel in your chosen niche.

Discussing Market Demand: Where Opportunities Are Brewing

The AI job market is as lively as a stock exchange floor, with certain specializations seeing more demand based on industry trends and technological advancements. For instance, as businesses increasingly rely on data-driven decisions, the demand for Machine Learning Engineers has skyrocketed. Similarly, with the growing awareness of AI's societal impact, the need for professionals in AI Ethics has surged.

Stay informed about market trends by subscribing to industry newsletters, attending webinars, and following influential figures in the AI community. Understanding where the demand is can help you tailor your learning and career strategy to fit the needs of the market, ensuring that your skills remain in high demand.

Advice on Specialization Transition: Charting Your Path in AI

Transitioning into an AI specialization is not unlike learning a new language. You might start with the basics, but immersion is key to becoming fluent. Begin by taking foundational courses in your chosen specialization. Platforms like Coursera or edX offer specialized courses that can introduce you to the fundamentals of fields like AI in Healthcare or Machine Learning.

Certifications can also add a feather to your cap, signaling your expertise to potential employers. Look for certification programs offered by reputable organizations or universities that provide hands-on learning experiences.

Gaining practical experience is crucial. Consider internships, project collaborations, or freelance opportunities that allow you to work on real-world problems in your chosen specialization. Each project enhances your understanding and adds to your portfolio, making you a more attractive candidate for future roles.

Remember, the world of AI is ever-evolving, and keeping pace with its changes requires an agile and proactive approach. By staying curious, continuously learning, and strategically positioning yourself in the AI landscape, you can not only find your niche but also thrive within it, shaping a career that is both rewarding and impactful.

7.3 Skills Development: Staying Relevant in the AI Job Market

As the AI landscape evolves at the speed of light, staying relevant is your ticket to thriving in this dynamic field. Imagine AI skills as your toolkit; without the right tools, or with outdated ones, you're going to find it tough to build anything worthwhile. So, let's gear up and ensure your AI toolkit is not only well-equipped but also sparkling new with the latest and greatest in technology.

Identifying Essential AI Skills: The Core of Your AI Arsenal

To navigate the AI job market, you'll need a blend of technical and soft skills. On the technical front, proficiency in programming languages like Python or R is non-negotiable. These are the chisels and hammers of AI work, allowing you to sculpt and build models from raw data. Then there's data analysis—a critical skill that helps you make sense of the numbers and trends before you even begin to think about algorithms.

But AI isn't just about number crunching; it's also about solving problems creatively. Problem-solving skills enable you to design and tweak AI models to address specific challenges, whether it's optimizing a supply chain or designing an algorithm that can predict market trends. And let's not forget communication, the golden thread that ties your technical prowess to the real world. Whether you're explaining a complex model to a non-tech-savvy stakeholder or writing clear documentation for your code, your ability to communicate clearly can make or break your effectiveness in an AI role.

Providing Learning Resources: Your Map to Mastery

Equipping yourself with these skills requires quality resources, and fortunately, the digital age is laden with learning gold. For programming and data analysis, platforms like Codecademy and DataCamp offer interactive courses that cover everything from basic Python to advanced machine learning algorithms. If you're looking to deepen your understanding of AI and machine learning, Coursera and edX feature courses designed by top universities like Stanford and MIT, often led by industry leaders and pioneers.

Books, too, can be an invaluable resource. Titles such as *Hands-On Machine Learning With Scikit-Learn, Keras, and TensorFlow* by Aurélien Géron offer practical insights and real-world examples that bridge theory with practice. For those who prefer a more structured learning environment, workshops and seminars—available both online and offline—provide opportunities not only to learn but also to network with peers and experts.

Emphasizing Adaptability and Innovation: Keeping Pace with AI

In the realm of AI, resting on your laurels is akin to walking on a treadmill—you might be moving, but you're not going anywhere. Adaptability and a knack for innovation are what keep you in stride with the ever-evolving technology. This means continuously updating your skills and staying open to new ways of thinking and solving problems. The AI field is known for its rapid adoption of new technologies; today's cutting-edge innovation could be tomorrow's old news.

Engage with the latest research, follow AI trends, and participate in forums and discussions. Platforms like arXiv and GitHub offer access to the latest research papers and projects in AI, providing a glimpse into the future of technology. Innovate by applying what you learn to new areas. For instance, if you've mastered machine learning techniques for financial forecasting, consider how those same techniques could be applied to predictive maintenance in manufacturing or to optimizing energy usage in smart grids.

Highlighting Skills Application: Turning Knowledge Into Action

Finally, the true test of your AI skills lies in their application. Real-world projects not only reinforce your learning but also demonstrate to potential employers that you can walk the AI walk, not just talk the talk. Participate in hackathons and competitions like those hosted on Kaggle, where you can tackle actual problems with your growing skillset. These platforms often provide problems sourced from industry, offering a realistic glimpse into the challenges businesses face and how AI can solve them.

Alternatively, consider contributing to open-source projects. These projects can be particularly rewarding as they offer a chance to work on software that might be used by millions, providing practical experience and improving your visibility in the AI community. For instance, contributing to a popular machine learning library like TensorFlow or PyTorch not only hones your skills but also helps you make a name for yourself in the field.

By continuously developing your skills, seeking out quality learning resources, embracing adaptability, and applying your knowledge to real-world projects, you ensure that your career in AI is not just sustainable but also successful and fulfilling. Remember, in the fast-paced world of AI, staying relevant is about being proactive, resourceful, and, above all, willing to learn and adapt.

7.4 Transitioning Into AI From Other Tech Fields

Imagine you're an experienced tech professional, comfortably navigating through code, networks, or data. One morning, over your third cup of coffee, you stumble upon an article about AI transforming lives and industries. A spark ignites; you're intrigued and ready to pivot your career towards AI. This isn't just about switching desks or tools—it's about embracing a field that's shaping the future. Let's walk through the process of transitioning from other tech fields into AI, ensuring you're equipped for this exciting shift.

Outline the Transition Process: Crafting Your AI Blueprint

The transition to AI can often feel like trying to solve a Rubik's cube—it's about aligning many elements perfectly. The first step is self-assessment; evaluate your current tech skills and understanding. Are you a software developer versed in Python? That's a plus since Python is a cornerstone in AI programming. Maybe you're a data analyst; your prowess in handling data can be a significant advantage in AI. Identify these transferable skills because they're your passport to AI.

Next, pinpoint the gaps. AI demands a unique blend of skills to master everything from machine learning to neural networks. Identify what you need to learn and start filling those gaps. For instance, if your background is in web development, you might need to deepen your knowledge in statistics and probability, which are crucial for understanding algorithms in machine learning.

Choosing the right learning path is paramount. Start with foundational courses in AI and machine learning available on platforms like Coursera or edX. These platforms offer courses designed by top universities and can provide both theoretical grounding and practical experience through projects. Also, consider specialized courses that can help you dive deeper into areas like deep learning or AI ethics, depending on your interests and career goals.

Leveraging Existing Skills: Turning Your Tech Toolbox Into an AI Kit

Your journey into AI doesn't mean leaving all your previous tech experience behind. In fact, many of the skills you've honed over the years will be invaluable as you transition into AI. For software developers, your coding skills will be crucial. AI development involves a lot of coding, whether you're writing algorithms from scratch or using frameworks like TensorFlow or PyTorch. Your experience in debugging, maintaining code, and version control are equally important in AI.

For those in data-related fields, your analytical skills are a gold mine. AI heavily relies on data—collecting, analyzing, and deriving insights from it. Your ability to manipulate and extract value from data can give you a head start in AI fields like data science or machine learning, where data preprocessing and feature extraction are critical tasks.

Even if your background is in less directly related fields like network administration, your understanding of complex systems, attention to detail, and project management skills will serve you well in AI. Transitioning involves retooling your existing skills to meet AI's demands but also appreciating how these competencies give you a unique edge in this new landscape.

Discussing Challenges and Solutions: Navigating New Territories

Transitioning into AI isn't without its hurdles. One common challenge is the steep learning curve. AI encompasses a broad range of complex topics that can be daunting. The key here is structured learning. Break down your learning goals into manageable parts and focus on one area at a time. Online communities and forums can also provide support and answer questions as you learn.

Another challenge is the cultural shift. AI often requires a different approach to problem-solving and project management. If you're used to very structured environments, the experimental and iterative nature of AI projects might be a shift. Engage with the community, find mentors, and immerse yourself in AI culture through meetups and conferences. This exposure can ease the cultural transition and help you adapt more quickly to new ways of working.

Lastly, mastering unfamiliar AI tools and platforms can be overwhelming. Start with one tool or platform. Many AI tools have robust documentation and active user communities, which can be invaluable resources as you learn. Online tutorials and courses can also provide guided learning to help you become proficient more quickly.

Featuring Transition Success Stories: From Peers to Pioneers

Consider the story of Maria, a network engineer with a decade of experience. Fascinated by the potential of AI in cybersecurity, she began her transition by taking online courses in machine learning. She leveraged her background in network security to focus on AI applications in anomaly detection, gradually building projects that showcased her growing expertise. Today, Maria leads the AI cybersecurity team at her company, blending her deep knowledge of networks with cutting-edge AI to enhance security protocols.

Then there's Alex, who transitioned from a career in database management to AI-driven data analytics. Alex started by using his SQL skills to clean and organize data for machine learning models. Through continuous learning and project work, he became proficient in Python and machine learning, eventually moving into a role where he now designs data strategies for AI applications in retail, helping companies personalize customer experiences based on big data insights.

These stories highlight not only the possibilities within AI but also the practical steps and strategies that can help you navigate this transition. They underscore an essential truth: With the right approach, transitioning into AI is not just a dream but a feasible step forward in your tech career. So, why wait? The future of AI beckons, and it's time to bring your tech skills into this exciting realm, where every line of code, every dataset, and every project can contribute to innovations that could reshape the world.

7.5 The Importance of Continuous Learning in AI Careers

The world of Artificial Intelligence is not just evolving; it's doing so at warp speed, making the Red Queen's race in *Alice in Wonderland* look like a leisurely stroll. To not only keep up but thrive in such a rapidly advancing field, adopting a lifelong learning mindset isn't just beneficial—it's imperative. Think of AI as an ever-expanding universe with constantly emerging new stars and planets. Staying updated with the latest discoveries and technological advancements in this cosmos requires an insatiable curiosity and an unwavering commitment to learning.

Embrace Continuous Learning: Your Career Lifeline

In AI, the learning never stops. This is not an overstatement but a stark reality of the field. Whether you're a neophyte stepping into the world of algorithms or a seasoned data scientist, the learning curve continues to steepen with the introduction of new technologies, theories, and tools. Embracing a mindset that views education as a continuous, integral part of your career is crucial. This mindset ensures you remain not only relevant but also competitive in a field where yesterday's innovations are just stepping stones for tomorrow's breakthroughs.

Consider the rapid advancements in areas like quantum computing, neuromorphic hardware, or GANs (generative adversarial networks). Each of these subfields can dramatically alter AI applications and capabilities. Staying abreast of such changes isn't just about adding new certificates to your wall—it's about deeply understanding how foundational shifts can impact your work and the broader implications for the industries you serve.

Diverse Avenues for Continuous Learning: Mapping Your Educational Journey

The paths to continuous learning in AI are as varied as the applications of AI itself. Formal education, such as master's degrees or PhD programs, offer depth and structured learning, but they aren't the only avenues. The digital age brings a plethora of learning platforms to your fingertips. Online courses from platforms like Udacity, Coursera, or Khan Academy provide flexibility and breadth, covering everything from basic programming to complex AI concepts like deep learning.

Workshops and conferences serve dual purposes; they are not only crucibles of learning but also melting pots of networking opportunities. Events like NeurIPS, ICML, or local meetups keep you updated on cutting-edge research and connect you with fellow AI enthusiasts and potential collaborators. Each interaction, each session attended, and each paper discussed at these gatherings could be the spark for your next project or the solution to a problem you've been wrestling with.

Moreover, the dynamic nature of AI makes it a perfect candidate for collaborative learning environments. Hackathons, coding camps, and team-based learning projects encourage hands-on experience with real-world data and problems. These settings not only challenge your coding skills but also your ability to work in teams and solve problems under pressure, mirroring the real challenges you'll face in the industry.

Engaging in Research and Development: Contributing to the AI Frontier

For those drawn to the thrill of innovation and discovery, participating in research and development provides a fulfilling avenue to contribute to the AI community. Engaging in R&D isn't confined to academia or corporate tech labs; it's increasingly accessible through open-source projects and collaborative research platforms. Contributing to projects on GitHub, participating in crowd-sourced research, or publishing findings in open-access journals like arXiv are all ways to contribute to the collective knowledge base of AI.

These activities allow you to apply theoretical knowledge in practical, often groundbreaking ways. They also elevate your profile in the AI community, establishing you as a thought leader and innovator. Whether it's improving the functionality of an open-source machine learning library or publishing a paper on novel uses of AI in environmental conservation, each contribution helps drive the field forward.

Crafting Professional Development Plans: Structuring Your Growth

Navigating continuous learning requires a blend of enthusiasm and strategy. Developing a professional development plan tailored to your career goals in AI can provide structure and clarity to your learning endeavors. Such plans should identify key skills gaps, set short and long-term learning objectives, and outline the resources needed to achieve these goals. Whether it's mastering a new programming language in six months or contributing to a major AI project within a year, having clear milestones and checkpoints can keep your learning on track.

Moreover, these plans should be dynamic, evolving as you progress in your career and as new trends emerge in AI. Regularly revisiting and revising your development plan is essential, ensuring it remains aligned with your career aspirations and the needs of the industry. This iterative process not only helps you stay focused but also ensures your learning efforts are intentional and aligned with your career trajectory.

In the relentless race of technological innovation, continuous learning is your most reliable engine. It propels not only your personal growth but also your professional advancement in the ever-evolving field of AI. By embracing a learning mindset, exploring diverse educational avenues, engaging in research and development, and strategically planning your professional development, you ensure that your career in AI is not just a fleeting sprint but a marathon of meaningful contributions and sustained success.

7.6 Networking and Community Engagement in the AI Industry

Imagine the AI industry as a vibrant marketplace where ideas, like exotic spices, are traded freely among enthusiasts, experts, and novices alike. In this environment, networking isn't just a beneficial activity—it's the currency that can buy you valuable opportunities, insights, and collaborations. Whether it's landing a dream job, finding the perfect collaborator for a groundbreaking project, or simply keeping your finger on the pulse of AI innovations, the art of networking can catapult your career to new heights.

The Golden Lure of Networking: Why It's Your Career Superpower

Networking in the AI industry is akin to planting seeds in a fertile field—the more you sow, the richer the harvest. It's about cultivating relationships that provide mutual benefits over time. These connections can lead to job opportunities that are often not advertised, giving you a leg up in the fiercely competitive job market. Collaborations can also stem from a simple conversation at an AI conference or a discussion on an online forum, leading to partnerships that combine diverse skills and ideas to create innovative solutions.

Moreover, networking is your telescope to the horizon of industry trends. By connecting with peers and leaders in the field, you gain insights into emerging technologies and shifts in the AI landscape, which can influence your career decisions and areas of focus. It's not just about who you know; it's about what you know through them, which can often be your greatest strategic advantage.

Crafting Effective Networking Strategies: How to Weave Your Web

The key to effective networking involves more than just attending events; you must engage meaningfully. Start by marking your presence at AI-related events like conferences, seminars, and workshops. These are gold mines for networking, offering you a platform to meet like-minded individuals who share your passion for AI. However, the secret sauce is in how you engage. Be genuinely interested in learning from others, ask insightful questions, and share your knowledge and experiences. It's about creating dialogues that are enriching for both parties, turning brief interactions into lasting connections.

Online platforms like LinkedIn and GitHub are also pivotal in your networking arsenal. They allow you to showcase your projects, achievements, and insights, attracting potential employers or collaborators. Engage regularly by sharing articles, joining discussions, and connecting with industry leaders whose work you admire. These platforms are not just about displaying your resume; they are dynamic ecosystems where ongoing engagement can lead to meaningful professional relationships.

Fostering Community Involvement: Beyond Networking Events

Joining AI communities, both online and offline, can significantly amplify your networking efforts. Forums, tech meetups, and hackathons not only bolster your understanding of AI but also embed you deeper within the network of AI professionals. Participating actively in these communities by contributing to discussions, volunteering for events, or presenting your work can enhance your visibility and establish you as a committed member of the AI community.

These communities often act as support systems where you can seek advice, evaluate ideas, and learn from the experiences of others. They provide a sense of belonging and can be particularly beneficial in staying motivated and connected, especially when navigating the complexities of a career in AI.

The Art of Finding and Leveraging Mentorship: Guided Pathways in AI

Mentorship in AI can be a game changer, providing you with guidance, feedback, and insights that are tailored to your personal and professional growth. Finding a mentor involves identifying someone whose career trajectory aligns with your aspirations or whose work inspires you. Engage with potential mentors at events, through professional platforms, or within your workplace. When reaching out, be clear about what you admire in their work and what guidance you are seeking.

Effective mentorship is a two-way street. It requires commitment, respect, and active engagement from both the mentor and the mentee. Set clear goals for what you wish to achieve through the mentorship, be open to feedback, and take proactive steps to act on the guidance you receive. This relationship can provide you with invaluable insights into navigating career challenges, making strategic decisions, and accessing opportunities that can propel your career forward.

In conclusion, networking and community engagement are indispensable elements of building a successful career in AI. They enable you to navigate the industry with an insider's advantage, leverage collective intelligence, and accelerate your career growth through meaningful connections and mentorship. As you step into the interconnected world of AI, remember that every handshake, every conversation, and every connection is a potential gateway to new horizons. Let these interactions be your stepping stones as you forge a path toward achieving your AI aspirations and carry these networking superpowers into the next chapter of your AI journey.

FUTURE TRENDS AND INNOVATIONS IN AI

Chapter 8

Future Trends and Innovations in AI

8.1 Quantum Computing and its Impact on AI

Step into the quantum realm, where the usual rules of computing bow down to the bizarre and bewildering laws of quantum mechanics. Here, in this *Alice in Wonderland* world of subatomic particles, quantum computing (QC) emerges not just as a new technology but as a revolution in creation, poised to turbocharge AI capabilities beyond our wildest imaginations.

Introducing Quantum Computing: Unraveling the Quantum Fabric

Quantum computing isn't just your regular upgrade—it's computing reimagined at the atomic level. At the heart of QC are principles like superposition and entanglement. Forget the classical bit that stores information as 0s or 1s; quantum bits, or qubits, can exist in both states simultaneously, thanks to superposition. This is a groundbreaking ability that allows quantum computers to process a vast number of possibilities simultaneously.

Entanglement, another quantum quirk, allows qubits that are entangled to instantly affect each other, regardless of the distance separating them. This spooky action at a distance (as Einstein famously put it) enables quantum computers to perform complex calculations at speeds unattainable by their classical counterparts, making them particularly promising for tasks that involve analyzing huge datasets or solving intricate optimization problems.

Potential in AI: Quantum Speed in an AI World

The synergy between quantum computing and AI is like the combination of peanut butter and jelly. On their own, each is impressive, but together, they're a powerhouse. Quantum computing could significantly enhance AI's ability to learn and make decisions, making it particularly potent for areas like machine learning, where algorithms improve their performance as they are exposed to more data.

Imagine AI models that currently take days to train on classical computers being trained in just hours or even minutes. Quantum algorithms are poised to accelerate deep learning processes, enhance reinforcement learning, and boost AI's capability in pattern recognition—think facial recognition or anomaly detection in cybersecurity.

Current Research and Experiments: Quantum Leaps on the Horizon

The landscape of quantum AI research is vibrant and bustling with activity. Institutions like Google's Quantum AI lab and IBM's Q Network are at the forefront, conducting experiments that integrate quantum computing with AI. Google's quantum processor, Sycamore, claimed "quantum supremacy" by performing a specific task in 200 seconds, which would otherwise take a supercomputer about 10,000 years.

These experiments aren't just about speed; they're about opening new pathways for AI applications. From optimizing traffic flows in mega-cities to finding new materials for clean energy technology, the potential applications for quantum-enhanced AI are as vast as they are impactful.

Challenges and Timelines: Quantum Hurdles Ahead

Despite its potential, quantum computing isn't ready for prime time—yet. The field faces significant technological and logistical challenges, from creating stable qubits that don't lose their quantum state (a problem known as decoherence) to scaling up the number of qubits to practical levels. Current quantum computers are more akin to sophisticated prototypes, demonstrating potential rather than ready-to-deploy solutions.

The timeline for when quantum computing will be routinely used in AI is still a matter of some debate. Most experts predict that it could take another decade or more to solve the fundamental challenges of making reliable, large-scale quantum computers. But as research continues and as we begin to understand more about leveraging quantum principles effectively, the integration of quantum computing in AI will likely become a game-changing reality.

So, as you navigate your AI career or continue your studies, keep an eye on the quantum horizon. The fusion of quantum computing and AI might still be in its infancy, but its progress will undoubtedly shape the future of technology, offering new tools and capabilities that today we can only imagine. Welcome to the quantum leap in AI—a journey into the heart of computing's most thrilling frontier.

8.2 The Next Generation of AI: Predictive Models and Their Evolution

Let's pull back the curtain on the evolution of predictive models, an epic saga that transforms from the simplicity of linear regressions to the sophistication of neural networks. Imagine early statisticians wielding linear regressions like blunt tools, carving out predictions in broad strokes. Fast forward, and the landscape is dominated by neural networks and machine learning, crafting finely-tuned predictions with the precision of a master sculptor.

The leap from linear to logistic regression was the first major plot twist in our story. Logistic regression, unlike its linear counterpart, could handle the messiness of categorizing outcomes—think of it as learning to predict whether it will rain, rather than predicting how much rain will fall. The plot thickens with the introduction of decision trees, random forests, and support vector machines, each method adding layers of complexity and accuracy to the model's ability to decipher patterns and predict outcomes.

Enter neural networks, the heavyweights of predictive modeling. With their deep layers and ability to learn from vast amounts of data, they changed the game. These networks don't just predict; they infer, adapt, and evolve. By mimicking the human brain's structure—neurons connected by synapses—they process data through layers to identify and amplify even the most subtle signals. Today, the fusion of neural networks with machine learning has spawned algorithms capable of predicting everything from stock market trends to medical diagnoses with astonishing accuracy.

Integration of AI With Predictive Analytics: Supercharging Forecasting Engines

As AI technologies cozy up to predictive analytics, they're turning traditional forecasting into a powerhouse capable of insights once thought impossible. In finance, AI-enhanced predictive models now forecast market movements with a precision that makes traditional methods look like ancient astrology. By analyzing patterns across vast datasets—incorporating everything from global economic indicators to Twitter sentiments—these models offer predictions that are not only about likely outcomes but also about the volatility and risk associated with these outcomes.

Healthcare, too, is experiencing a revolution. AI-driven predictive models help forecast patient outcomes, personalize treatment plans, and even predict epidemic outbreaks. By integrating patient data, treatment histories, and genetic information, these models can anticipate health issues before they manifest, significantly improving preventive care.

Retail isn't left behind; it's being transformed by AI that predicts purchasing trends, optimizes inventory, and personalizes marketing to match an individual's buying habits. Imagine walking into a store where the offers you see are aligned perfectly with your preferences, thanks to predictive analytics working silently in the background, analyzing your past purchases and browsing habits.

Future Potential of Predictive AI: The Crystal Ball of Technology

Looking ahead, the potential of predictive AI stretches even further. Real-time analytics are on the horizon, promising the ability to make predictions on-the-fly. This technology could dynamically adjust traffic light sequences to prevent congestion based on real-time traffic data or instantly recommend a personalized marketing offer as soon as a customer interacts with a product online.

Predictive maintenance is another frontier, particularly in manufacturing and aviation, where AI models predict equipment failures before they occur. This not only saves on costly repairs but also significantly reduces downtime, boosting productivity. In healthcare, personalized predictive models are set to revolutionize treatment by using ongoing personal health data to continuously update and refine individual health predictions and treatment plans.

Impact on Decision-Making: Steering the Ship With Data-Driven Strategies

The ripple effect of improved predictive models on decision-making is profound. Businesses and governments are increasingly shifting towards data-driven strategies, where decisions are guided by predictive insights rather than gut feelings or historical precedents. This shift isn't just about efficiency; it's about effectiveness, precision, and the ability to anticipate and mitigate risks before they become problems.

In governance, predictive AI can lead to more informed policy-making. For instance, by predicting economic trends, governments can better prepare for downturns with proactive measures. In business, executives can use predictive insights to strategize market entries, product developments, and competitive tactics with a level of precision that was previously the domain of fortune tellers.

As we stand on the brink of these advancements, the integration of AI with predictive analytics is not just enhancing our ability to forecast; it's redefining what it means to anticipate the future. Whether it's in finance, healthcare, retail, or beyond, predictive AI is setting the stage for a world where the future isn't just something to be experienced but something to be shaped.

Deepen your understanding of neural networks, support vectors, and decision trees with ML Playground's interactive exercises:

8.3 AI and the Internet of Things: A Converging Future

Imagine a world where your coffee maker knows just when to have your morning brew ready, or your office dynamically adjusts its temperature based on how many people are present. Welcome to the integrated universe of AI and the Internet of Things (IoT), where smart devices don't just function—they learn, adapt, and make decisions. This integration is transforming everyday objects into active participants in our daily lives, enhancing efficiency, safety, and sustainability across various domains.

Defining the Integration: Smarter Devices, Smarter Decisions

The fusion of AI with IoT is like giving brains to inanimate objects. IoT refers to the vast network of devices connected to the internet, collecting and exchanging data. Now, inject AI into this network, and these devices can analyze this data, learn from it, and make decisions without human intervention. For instance, AI in a smart thermostat learns from your preferences and adjusts the temperature automatically, optimizing comfort and energy use over time. It's not just about connectivity; it's about making these connections intelligent.

The magic happens through machine learning algorithms that allow devices to recognize patterns and make predictions. Consider a security camera with AI capabilities. Traditional cameras record footage, but AI-enhanced cameras can identify whether the movement detected is a burglar or just the neighbor's cat exploring your garden. By processing data at the source, AI-enabled IoT devices reduce the need to transmit vast amounts of data to the cloud, enhancing response times and reducing bandwidth usage.

Real-World Applications: Enhancing Lives and Industries

The practical applications of AI-enhanced IoT are as varied as they are impactful. In smart homes, devices that adjust lighting, heating, and security settings not only offer convenience but also improve energy efficiency and reduce costs. In industrial settings, the integration of AI with IoT—often termed Industrial IoT (IIoT)—transforms operations. Sensors with AI capabilities in manufacturing equipment capabilities predict equipment failures before they occur, allowing for timely maintenance that minimizes downtime and extends the equipment's life.

Smart cities represent another transformative application. AI-powered IoT devices manage everything from traffic systems that adapt to real-time road conditions, reducing congestion and pollution, to smart grids that optimize electricity distribution based on real-time demand and supply data. These applications not only improve city living conditions but also contribute to substantial economic and environmental benefits.

Challenges in Integration: Navigating the Complexities

However, integrating AI with IoT is not without its challenges. Scalability tops the list. As the number of smart devices rapidly grows, so does the strain on the networks that connect them. Ensuring these networks can handle vast amounts of data without lagging is crucial. Security is another significant concern. With devices interconnected, a single vulnerability can jeopardize the entire network. Ensuring robust security protocols that can evolve with emerging threats is paramount.

Data privacy also poses a major challenge. With devices constantly collecting and analyzing data, ensuring this data is used ethically and in compliance with privacy laws is a critical concern for developers and users alike. Developing frameworks that protect user data without hindering the functionality of smart devices requires a delicate balance and is an ongoing area of focus in the development of AI-enhanced IoT.

Vision for the Future: A Smart, Connected World

Looking to the future, the potential innovations in AI-powered IoT devices are boundless. Imagine smart cities with AI-driven public services that are not only automated but also predictive, capable of identifying and addressing issues, from traffic jams to public safety concerns, before they escalate. Consider the advancements in healthcare, where AI-enhanced wearable devices monitor health metrics so they can predict potential health issues before they become critical, offering a new dimension to preventative care.

The ongoing advancements in AI and machine learning algorithms will continue to push the boundaries of what's possible in IoT. As these technologies mature and their integration deepens, the future points to an increasingly interconnected world. This convergence promises to streamline and enhance many aspects of daily life and industry operations; it will also bring about significant societal transformations, characterized by unprecedented levels of efficiency, safety, and sustainability. As we continue to innovate and navigate the challenges, the journey towards a fully intelligent and connected world is not just a possibility but an impending reality.

8.4 Ethical AI Development: Emerging Standards and Practices

As we march forward into the age of artificial intelligence, the buzz isn't just about what AI can do—it's increasingly about how AI should do it. The ethical stakes are high, and the call for responsible AI development has echoed across boardrooms, parliaments, and living rooms around the world. Emerging ethical standards and practices in AI aren't just footnotes in tech manuals; they are becoming the bedrock upon which sustainable innovation in AI is built.

Emerging Ethical Standards: Crafting the Moral Compass of AI

Global organizations and governments are not merely spectators but active participants in shaping the ethical landscape of AI. Initiatives such as the EU's Ethics Guidelines for Trustworthy AI set out requirements that AI systems should meet to be deemed trustworthy, including transparency, fairness, and accountability. Similarly, the IEEE's Global Initiative on Ethics of Autonomous and Intelligent Systems offers comprehensive guidelines that cover ethical design for AI, underscoring the importance of aligning AI development with human values and ethical principles.

These ethical frameworks are not static; they evolve as our understanding of AI's impact deepens. They serve a dual purpose: safeguarding societal values and fostering public trust in AI technologies. By establishing clear guidelines, these initiatives help demystify the ethical expectations for AI developers and users, ensuring that AI innovations enhance societal well-being without crossing ethical boundaries.

Role of Ethics in Innovation: The Ethical Engine of AI Progress

One might wonder, does focusing on ethics stifle innovation? The answer is quite the contrary. Integrating ethical considerations into AI development is proving to be a catalyst for more sustainable and widely accepted AI solutions. Ethical AI is not about putting up roadblocks; it's about steering innovation in a direction that maximizes benefits while minimizing harm.

162

Ethics drive innovation by prompting developers to think creatively about how to achieve performance goals without compromising on values such as privacy and fairness. This can lead to breakthroughs in AI technology, such as the development of new algorithms that provide transparency about their decision-making processes or models that can be easily audited for bias and fairness. Moreover, ethical AI practices attract public support and acceptance, crucial for the widespread adoption of new technologies.

Case Studies: Ethical AI in Action

Consider the case of a tech company that implemented AI to streamline its hiring process. Initially, the AI system was biased against certain demographic groups. Recognizing this, the company used guidelines from ethical AI frameworks to redesign the system. This involved retraining the AI with a more diverse dataset and adjusting the algorithm to ensure fairness in candidate selection. The result was a more equitable hiring process that not only improved the company's diversity but also enhanced its reputation and employee satisfaction.

Another example comes from the healthcare sector, where an AI application was developed to assist with patient diagnosis. The developers integrated ethical guidelines right from the start, focusing on transparency and user consent. The AI system was designed to explain its diagnostic recommendations to both patients and doctors, ensuring that the decision-making process was transparent. This build-up of trust led to higher acceptance of the AI system, ultimately improving patient outcomes and operational efficiency in the hospital.

Future of AI Ethics: Anticipating Self-Regulating AI

Looking ahead, the frontier of AI ethics includes the tantalizing prospect of AI systems that can autonomously ensure their actions remain within ethical boundaries. Imagine AI systems equipped with "ethical governors" that continuously assess and align the system's actions with established ethical guidelines. Such self-regulating AI could dynamically adjust its operations in response to ethical considerations, potentially revolutionizing how AI systems are integrated into sensitive areas like healthcare and law enforcement.

Moreover, as AI systems become more capable of handling complex tasks, the development of adaptive ethical guidelines that can evolve in response to new challenges and scenarios will be crucial. These guidelines would not be rigid but would adapt based on real-world experiences and emerging ethical insights.

As we navigate these developments, the role of ethics in AI continues to be a beacon that guides the technology's evolution. It ensures that as AI systems become more integrated into our daily lives, they do so in a way that respects human values and promotes societal well-being. The future of ethical AI development promises not only smarter AI but also a more humane and just technological future.

8.5 AI in Space Exploration: Opportunities and Challenges

Venture beyond Earth's atmosphere, and the role of artificial intelligence (AI) in space exploration becomes as clear as the night sky. Far from being just another tool, AI has become integral in interpreting the vast data cosmos collected by telescopes and satellites, navigating rovers across alien terrains, and maintaining spacecraft far from human reach. This stellar integration of AI in the final frontier is not just about pushing boundaries; it's about redefining them.

AI Applications in Space: Navigating the Cosmic Seas

Consider the sophisticated telescopes peering into the depths of space, capturing more data in a day than we could analyze in a lifetime. Here,

AI steps in as the ultimate cosmic librarian, sifting through petabytes of data to detect patterns and anomalies that the human eye might miss. This isn't just about spotting new stars or galaxies; it's about understanding cosmic phenomena like black holes and neutron stars, or catching the faint, telltale signs of planets orbiting distant stars. AI's ability to rapidly process and analyze this data is crucial for making timely scientific discoveries and deepening our understanding of the universe.

On the more rugged terrains of Mars, AI-driven rovers like NASA's Perseverance are tasked with navigating vast landscapes, analyzing geological formations, and searching for signs of past life. These rovers rely on AI for autonomous navigation, avoiding obstacles and making route decisions in real-time without waiting for instructions from Earth, where a single command can take minutes to arrive. This autonomy is crucial in environments where human pilotage is impractical, if not impossible.

Moreover, AI's role extends into the operational health of spacecraft. Predictive maintenance powered by AI algorithms can foresee potential failures in spacecraft systems by analyzing data trends and anomalies. This proactive approach to maintenance ensures that minor issues can be addressed before they evolve into critical failures, potentially saving multimillion-dollar missions and ensuring the safety and longevity of the spacecraft.

Collaboration Between AI and Astrobiology: Seeking Life Beyond Earth

Astrobiology, the study of life in the universe, has found a powerful ally in AI. As we search for extraterrestrial life, AI helps in analyzing the environmental data from other planets and moons to assess their habitability. By simulating planetary environments and running countless scenarios, AI helps scientists understand how life could potentially arise in conditions different from those on Earth.

AI's ability to sift through data extends to the search for biosignatures, the subtle hints of life that might be left behind in a planet's atmosphere or on its surface. For instance, AI algorithms process spectral data from telescopes to detect the presence of methane or oxygen in distant worlds; these gases could potentially indicate biological processes. This hunt for life isn't just a needle-in-a-haystack problem; it's a needle in a cosmic haystack, where AI's analytical prowess becomes indispensable.

Challenges in Space: AI Meets the Cosmic Void

Space is the ultimate test of resilience and ingenuity, presenting unique challenges for AI. The extreme conditions of space, characterized by severe temperature fluctuations, radiation levels, and the vacuum of space, pose significant risks to the hardware that AI systems depend on. AI algorithms must be robust enough to withstand these conditions, requiring special hardening of AI hardware against radiation and extreme temperatures.

Data transmission is another hurdle. The vast distance between interplanetary space missions and Earth means that communication delays are inevitable and data bandwidth is limited. AI's ability to make autonomous decisions is critically important in these scenarios, as real-time human oversight is not feasible. The data that AI systems collect must be prioritized and compressed intelligently for transmission back to Earth, ensuring that the most valuable insights don't get lost in the cosmic void.

Future Prospects: AI and the New Age of Cosmic Voyages

Looking to the horizon, the integration of AI in space exploration holds promises that could redefine humanity's future in space. AI could drive advancements in interstellar travel, allowing autonomous spacecraft to voyage beyond our solar system, navigate through interstellar space, and, perhaps one day, reach neighboring stars. These missions may rely entirely on AI for navigation, decision-making, and problem-solving, marking a new era of exploration where AI and robotics extend humanity's reach into the cosmos.

Moreover, as the scale of space missions grows, AI's role in managing complex, multi-platform missions involving swarms of satellites or a network of space stations will become increasingly crucial. Imagine a coordinated fleet of AI-guided vehicles on the Moon or Mars, conducting scientific research, building infrastructure, or mining resources, all operating harmoniously under the guidance of advanced AI systems.

In this expansive view, the future of space exploration with AI at the helm is not just about scientific discovery or technological prowess; it's about opening a gateway to the stars, where AI-enabled exploration crafts a new narrative in the human quest to understand and explore the universe. As we stand on this threshold, the cosmic dance between AI and space exploration continues, promising to unlock secrets of the cosmos that have captivated humanity since we first looked skyward.

8.6 The Future of AI Governance: What Lies Ahead

Navigating the labyrinth of AI governance feels akin to umpiring a game where the rules evolve with every play. As we stand amidst rapid technological advancements, AI governance remains a dynamic and crucial arena, necessitating a robust framework to ensure that the development and deployment of AI technologies not only foster innovation but also adhere to ethical and societal norms.

Current State of AI Governance: Navigating the Regulatory Maze

The landscape of AI governance today is a patchwork quilt, with each piece representing different national regulations, international agreements, and guidelines set forth by influential tech giants and academic entities. At the national level, countries like the United States, the European Union members, and China have developed their own AI governance frameworks, focusing on aspects ranging from privacy and data protection to intellectual property and cross-border data flows. These frameworks are crucial, yet they vary significantly, reflecting diverse legal, cultural, and political environments.

Internationally, organizations such as the United Nations and the OECD have been instrumental in shaping AI governance. These bodies have proposed frameworks and guidelines that emphasize AI's ethical implications, transparency, and accountability. The OECD's AI Principles, for instance, are endorsed by over 40 countries and aim to promote AI that is innovative and trustworthy and that respects human rights and democratic values.

However, the effectiveness of AI governance is often hampered by the pace of AI development. Regulations struggle to keep up with the rapid evolution of AI technologies, leading to gaps that can potentially be exploited. Moreover, the voluntary nature of many of these guidelines means that adherence is inconsistent, and enforcement mechanisms are often lacking.

Challenges in AI Governance: The Roadblocks Ahead

One of the most pressing challenges in AI governance is achieving international cooperation. AI technologies cross borders, making unilateral national policies insufficient and sometimes counterproductive. For instance, an AI application developed in one country can be deployed across the globe, potentially circumventing stricter regulatory environments. This necessitates international agreements to ensure a coherent approach to AI governance, yet achieving global consensus is a complex and often slow process.

The dizzying pace of AI innovation further complicates governance. AI technologies evolve at a speed that regulations simply cannot match. By the time a regulation is implemented, the technology it governs may have already advanced beyond the regulation's scope, rendering it obsolete. This lag poses significant challenges in creating and enforcing effective governance.

Moreover, enforcing these regulations poses its own set of challenges. The technical complexity of AI systems makes it difficult for regulators to understand and evaluate these technologies thoroughly. This is compounded by the shortage of technical expertise within regulatory bodies, making effective oversight challenging.

Proposals for Future Governance: Shaping a Cohesive Framework

Looking forward, several proposals aim to strengthen AI governance. One such proposal is the establishment of global AI watchdogs— bodies that would operate internationally to oversee AI development and deployment, ensuring compliance with agreed-upon standards and ethics. These entities would not only monitor but also have the authority to enforce regulations, bridging the gap between guidelines and actual practice.

Another innovative approach is the adoption of decentralized regulatory frameworks. Leveraging blockchain technology, these frameworks could provide a transparent and immutable record of AI systems' development and use, facilitating better compliance and accountability. Additionally, integrating AI systems into the regulatory processes themselves—using AI to monitor AI—could enhance oversight capabilities and responsiveness.

Finally, there's a growing call for regulations that are adaptive and iterative, capable of evolving alongside AI technologies. This could involve frameworks that are regularly updated through a collaborative process involving stakeholders from across the AI ecosystem, including technologists, policymakers, industry leaders, and civil society. Such a dynamic approach could help governance keep pace with technological advancements, ensuring that regulations remain relevant and effective.

Speculative Scenarios: Envisioning the Governance of Tomorrow

Envisioning the future of AI governance, we might see scenarios where AI plays a central role in its own regulation. Imagine AI systems equipped with built-in compliance mechanisms that automatically adjust their operations to align with changing regulations. On the flip side, overly stringent regulations could stifle innovation, leading to a slowdown in AI advancements and potentially causing a brain drain to more lenient jurisdictions.

Alternatively, a successful global governance framework could lead to a harmonized AI landscape, where technologies are developed and deployed safely and ethically across borders. This would not only enhance global cooperation but also foster a more equitable distribution of AI benefits.

As we navigate these possibilities, the path forward in AI governance will undoubtedly influence how technologies shape our world. Striking the right balance between innovation and regulation, and autonomy and oversight, will define the trajectory of AI development and its integration into society.

In wrapping up this exploration into the future of AI governance, it's clear that the journey ahead is both promising and fraught with challenges. The governance frameworks we establish today will lay the groundwork for the future, influencing how technologies evolve and how they're integrated into our daily lives. As we turn the page to the next chapter, the discussion shifts from the theoretical to the practical, examining real-world applications and the tangible impacts of AI across various sectors. Here, the abstract meets the concrete, and the policies and proposals discussed previously are put to the test in the bustling arenas of industry, healthcare, and beyond.

Conclusion

As we close this chapter—quite literally—on our exploration of the transformative journey of AI, let's take a moment to marvel at the evolution of artificial intelligence. From its humble beginnings as a mere concept of "thinking machines" to today's generative AI marvels, which can not only think but also create, it's been quite the saga. The trajectory of AI has been nothing short of a blockbuster, with twists and turns that have propelled industries from healthcare to entertainment into the future.

Reflecting on the core themes of this book, we've navigated through the dense forest of neural networks, dived deep into the oceans of machine learning, and scaled the mountains of ethical AI development. Each chapter has built upon the last, adding layers of understanding and sophistication to your AI knowledge arsenal.

From the foundational theories discussed in the early chapters to the advanced applications and ethical considerations tackled later on, the key takeaways have been manifold. We've seen how generative AI is not just about technology but about the potential to enhance human creativity and solve complex problems in ways that were previously unimaginable.

However, with great power comes great responsibility. The importance of steering AI development with a strong ethical compass cannot be overstated. As we stand on the brink of AI possibilities, it's crucial that these technologies are developed and used in ways that benefit society as a whole, respecting human rights and promoting well-being.

Now, as you step out from the pages of this book and back into the world, I urge you to keep the flame of curiosity burning. The field of AI is as dynamic as it is fascinating, and staying abreast of the latest research, tools, and ethical guidelines will be key to navigating its future landscapes. Whether you're a developer, a researcher, or simply an AI enthusiast, continuous learning will be your most valuable tool.

I call upon you, the reader, to take the insights and knowledge you've gained and apply them to your own AI endeavors. Experiment, innovate, and perhaps most importantly, consider the ethical implications of your work. The future of AI offers a canvas as vast as the imagination, and it is up to all of us to paint it wisely.

Looking ahead, I am filled with optimism. AI is poised to continue its trajectory of incredible growth, opening up new horizons that we are only beginning to conceive. It promises not only to augment human capabilities but also to offer new solutions to age-old challenges, making our world a smarter, more efficient, and more understanding place.

Thank you for joining me on this journey through the fascinating world of AI. It's been a privilege to share this guide with you. As you move forward, armed with new knowledge and perspectives, remember that the future of AI is not just something to be observed but to be shaped. Here's to shaping a future that reflects the best of technology and the best of humanity. Happy innovating!

Spread the word: If this book has given you insight, joy, or a fresh perspective on the exciting world of generative AI, a positive review on Amazon would be immensely appreciated. Your kind words could help others discover the countless benefits of AI within this book. **To leave a review, please scan the QR code below:**

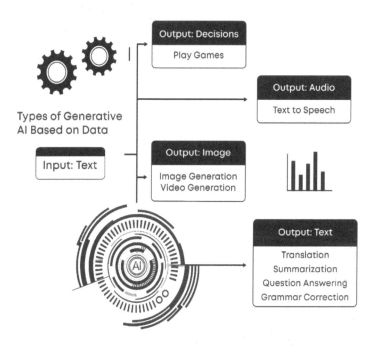

Types of Generative AI Based on Data

Input: Text

Output: Decisions
Play Games

Output: Audio
Text to Speech

Output: Image
Image Generation
Video Generation

Output: Text
Translation
Summarization
Question Answering
Grammar Correction

AI

References

AI model optimization: How to do it and why it matters. (n.d.). Enterprise AI.
https://www.techtarget.com/searchenterpriseai/tip/AI-model-
optimization-How-to-do-it-and-why-it-matters

Analytics Vidhya. (2019, November 20). *A comprehensive guide to attention mechanism in
deep learning.*
https://www.analyticsvidhya.com/blog/2019/11/comprehensive-guide-
attention-mechanism-deep-learning/

Arkenberg, C. (2023, June 29). *Generative AI is already disrupting media and entertainment.*
Deloitte Insights.
https://www2.deloitte.com/us/en/insights/industry/technology/generativ
e-ai-tools-media-entertainment.html

Baheti, P. (2021, July 8). *The essential guide to neural network architectures.*
www.v7labs.com. https://www.v7labs.com/blog/neural-network-
architectures-guide

Bland AI review: Unveiling the power of AI in call centers. (2024, January 9). Tasktwister.
https://tasktwister.com/ai/bland-ai-review-unveiling-the-power-of-ai-in-
call-centers-2024/

Budiu, R. (2018, November 25). The user experience of chatbots. Nielsen Norman
Group. https://www.nngroup.com/articles/chatbots/

Coursera. (2024, June 5). *Artificial intelligence (AI) career roadmap: Jobs and levels guide.*
https://www.coursera.org/resources/job-leveling-matrix-for-artificial-
intelligence-career-pathways

Data Summit Dublin. (2018, September 19). *Innovation and regulation online* [Video].
Data Summit Dublin. https://datasummitdublin.ie/

Davenport, T., & Kalakota, R. (2019). The potential for artificial intelligence in
healthcare. *Future Healthcare Journal, 6*(2), 94–98.
https://doi.org/10.7861/futurehosp.6-2-94

Deloitte. (2022). Preserving privacy in artificial intelligence applications through
anonymization of sensitive data preserving privacy in artificial intelligence
applications through anonymization of sensitive data.
https://www2.deloitte.com/content/dam/Deloitte/de/Documents/Innov

ation/Deloitte_Trustworthy%20AI%20_Data%20Anonymization_Feb2022
.pdf

Dey, S. (2023). *Council post: Which ethical implications of generative AI should companies focus on?* Forbes.
https://www.forbes.com/sites/forbestechcouncil/2023/10/17/which-ethical-implications-of-generative-ai-should-companies-focus-on/

Ethics of artificial intelligence. (2022). UNESCO. https://www.unesco.org/en/artificial-intelligence/recommendation-ethics

Exploring AI in web development: Future trends & Impacts. (n.d.). Changency.
https://www.changencydm.us/blog/the-impact-of-artificial-intelligence-on-web-development-enhancing-user-experience

Farhud, D. D., & Zokaei, S. (2021). Ethical issues of artificial intelligence in medicine and healthcare. *Iranian Journal of Public Health*, *50*(11).
https://doi.org/10.18502/ijph.v50i11.7600

Gomede, E. (2023, September 21). Understanding sequence-to-sequence (seq2seq) models and their significance. *Medium.*
https://medium.com/@evertongomede/understanding-sequence-to-sequence-seq2seq-models-and-their-significance-d2f0fd5f6f7f

GPT-3 powers the next generation of apps. (2021, March 25). OpenAI.
https://openai.com/index/gpt-3-apps/

Harrison, H. (2024, January 1). *Monthly market update: December.* Scoop by Shares.
https://blog.shares.io/news/stock-market-news/monthly-market-update-december/

How businesses use Google Cloud Vertex AI. (n.d.). Google Cloud Blog.
https://cloud.google.com/blog/products/ai-machine-learning/how-businesses-use-google-cloud-vertex-ai

IBM. (2015, October 1). *Why avoiding bias is critical to AI success | Building successful AI that's grounded in trust and transparency.* IBM.
https://www.ibm.com/resources/guides/predict/trustworthy-ai/avoid-bias/

Introduction - Hugging Face NLP course. (n.d.). Hugging Face.
https://huggingface.co/learn/nlp-course/chapter1/1

Kavanagh, C. (2019, August 28). *New tech, new threats, and new governance challenges: An opportunity to craft smarter responses?* Carnegie Endowment for International Peace – Papers. https://carnegieendowment.org/research/2019/08/new-tech-new-threats-and-new-governance-challenges-an-opportunity-to-craft-smarter-responses?lang=en

Lawton, G. (2023, April 18). *Generative AI ethics: 8 biggest concerns.* TechTarget. https://www.techtarget.com/searchenterpriseai/tip/Generative-AI-ethics-8-biggest-concerns

Lee, N. T., Resnick, P., & Barton, G. (2019, May 22). *Algorithmic bias detection and mitigation: Best practices and policies to reduce consumer harms.* Brookings. https://www.brookings.edu/articles/algorithmic-bias-detection-and-mitigation-best-practices-and-policies-to-reduce-consumer-harms/

Mahaffey, C.D. (2024, April 16. Mastering best practices in generative AI integration: A comprehensive guide. *Medium.* https://medium.com/@AIreporter/mastering-best-practices-in-generative-ai-integration-a-comprehensive-guide-aa82bd53c7c9

Mastering transformer architecture: Attention is all you need. (2024, March 28). MyScale. https://myscale.com/blog/understanding-transformer-architecture-attention-need/

McKinsey & Company. (2023, August 1). *The state of AI in 2023: Generative AI's breakout year.* McKinsey. https://www.mckinsey.com/capabilities/quantumblack/our-insights/the-state-of-ai-in-2023-generative ais-breakout-year

McKinsey & Company. (2023, June 15). *Economic potential of generative AI.* McKinsey. https://www.mckinsey.com/capabilities/mckinsey-digital/our-insights/the-economic-potential-of-generative-ai-the-next-productivity-frontier

Mentorship in the digital age: AI and virtual platforms for optimized career growth. (2023, October 18). HR Future. https://www.hrfuture.net/talent-management/personal-development/mentorship-in-the-digital-age-ai-and-virtual-platforms-for-optimized-career-growth/

Oliver, L. (2024, February 7). *Advancements and trends in the instrument transformer industry* [Post]. LinkedIn. https://www.linkedin.com/pulse/advancements-trends-instrument-transformer-industry-laila-oliver-dux9f#:~:text=Smart%20transformers%20equipped%20with%20sensors,the%20transition%20towards%20smart%20grids.

Oniwura, B. (2023, July 4). Film color grading and artificial intelligence. Medium. https://medium.com/@onigold2/film-color-grading-and-ai-939d5dc21c1c

PWC. (n.d.). *A practical guide to responsible artificial intelligence (AI).* https://www.pwc.com/gx/en/issues/data-and-analytics/artificial-intelligence/what-is-responsible-ai/responsible-ai-practical-guide.pdf

PyTorch - market share, competitor insights in data science and machine learning. (n.d.). 6sense. Retrieved July 9, 2024, from https://www.6sense.com/tech/data-science-machine-learning/pytorch-market-share

Rao, R. (n.d.). *Quantum computers can run powerful AI that works like the brain.* Scientific American. https://www.scientificamerican.com/article/quantum-computers-can-run-powerful-ai-that-works-like-the-brain/

Sanders, N. R., & Wood, J. D. (2023, November 3). *The skills your employees need to work effectively with AI.* Harvard Business Review. https://hbr.org/2023/11/the-skills-your-employees-need-to-work-effectively-with-ai

sitiatarfa8. (2024, January 18). *AI personalization: How eCommerce transform their business.* Kitameraki. https://www.kitameraki.com/post/how-shopee-and-others-transforming-ecommerce-with-ai-personalization-strategies

Smith, M. G. (2024, May 30). *Overcoming data privacy and security challenges in AI deployment.* CalypsoAI. https://calypsoai.com/overcoming-data-privacy-and-security-challenges-in-ai-deployment/

Zayed, M. (2023, November 28). Understanding neural networks: A comprehensive guide. DEV Community. https://dev.to/mariazayed/understanding-neural-networks-a-comprehensive-guide-28cg

Zhuraval, H. (n.d.). *AI and IoT: Exploring a powerful technological synergy.* Binariks. https://binariks.com/blog/ai-iot-use-cases-and-benefits/

Made in United States
Troutdale, OR
04/18/2025